v be kept

GREEK PIETY

GREEK PIETY

BY

MARTIN PERSSON NILSSON

PROFESSOR EMERITUS OF CLASSICAL ARCHAEOLOGY
UNIVERSITY OF LUND, SWEDEN

TRANSLATED
FROM THE SWEDISH BY

HERBERT JENNINGS ROSE

PROFESSOR OF GREEK, ST. ANDREWS UNIVERSITY

OXFORD
AT THE CLARENDON PRESS

Oxford University Press, Amen House, London E.C. 4

GLASGOW NEW YORK TORONTO MELBOURNE WELLINGTON
BOMBAY CALCUTTA MADRAS CAPE TOWN

Geoffrey Cumberlege, Publisher to the University

FIRST EDITION 1948
Reprinted lithographically in Great Britain
at the UNIVERSITY PRESS, OXFORD, 1951
by Charles Batey, Printer to the University
from sheets of the first edition

TRANSLATOR'S PREFACE

PROFESSOR NILSSON, thanks to his enviable command of modern languages, needs no introduction to a British or American audience. In the present book he has summed up the results of a lifetime of research into the many fascinating problems presented by ancient religion, and has turned his attention not so much to what the ancients at various dates did and said as to the feelings which prompted them, and the beliefs, expressed or implied, which underlay their ritual. Of the facts adduced, not many are unfamiliar to those who have given any attention to the subject, though even here all but the most expert will probably find something new to them; the novelty is in the interpretation, especially of the relation of Christianity to the other and competing religions which coexisted with the age of its growth and expansion. Here the most learned will find something to stimulate them and, if they chance to disagree, to suggest further and fruitful investigation.

My task, and it has proved both pleasant and profitable, has been simply to say in plain English what the author had set down in good Swedish. The translations, be they good or bad, of quotations from ancient authors are my own, made from the original Greek or Latin, except part of the extract from Pindar on p. 55, which was rendered by Professor Cornford and originally appeared in the English version of the same author's treatise on the *History of Greek Religion*, p. 226, and the Biblical citations, which are taken from the Authorized Version. Passages from the choruses of Greek plays are turned in an imitation of the metres of the original.

A word as to the title. In Swedish it is *Grekisk religiositet*, and the word *religiositet* recurs frequently in the text. To translate this by 'religiosity' would have been quite impossible, for that word, in English, has a depreciatory meaning which is wholly wanting in its Swedish (and German) use. In the text I have used 'religious feeling' generally, sometimes simply 'religion'; for the title I decided on 'Greek Piety', which does not pretend to be exact, for 'piety' is not *religiositet* but *fromhet*, yet it seems to me to denote the content of the work clearly enough.

H. J. R.

st. andrews,
    June 1947

AUTHOR'S PREFACE

SO many books, excellent in their kind, have been published on Greek religion in recent years, that it may be asked if there is room for another. I hope, however, that this book deserves its place because of its special character. It has not much to say of the religion of great writers and of philosophers, still less of gods and their cult, but its aim is to set forth the religious attitude towards the world and the religious view of the life of man, as these changed with the times. It perhaps will also be understood that the writer, who has devoted a large part of his long life to studying the religion of Greece, wishes to state in broad outline the results at which he believes he has arrived, in a form more generally intelligible because not weighted with the detailed discussions and learned apparatus which are necessary in a strictly scientific and thorough treatment. For all such matters reference is made to my *Geschichte der griechischen Religion*, of which the first volume came out in 1941 and the second is ready in manuscript, to be published as soon as circumstances allow. My warmest thanks are due to Professor Rose for his readiness to undertake the translation. His name on the title-page will recommend my book to English readers.

M. P. N.

LUND, *May* 1946

CONTENTS

INTRODUCTION

THE NATIONAL RELIGION OF GREECE

THE ancient religion of Greece has been portrayed by eminent investigators, who have thrown light on it from different angles. Some have directed their attention to the lofty religious ideas of the great poets and the deep thoughts of the philosophers concerning gods and the life of men. But the poets were makers of poetry, not religious reformers; what a Pindar or an Aeschylus says of gods and divine governance left hardly a trace in the religion of their own day or of later times. The philosophers were seekers after truth and men of science, and while certain movements within philosophy did much in classical times to break down religious belief, a matter to which we will return later on, philosophy did nothing to construct belief or religious opinion until the Hellenistic age. That is true especially of Stoicism, but even for the Stoics religious speculation was far from being the principal task, although they were more and more inclined to explain and defend religion and its forms. Plato was one of the greatest religious geniuses of all time, but he regarded himself, and was regarded by his contemporaries, as a philosopher, a seeker after truth, and a man of science. The view he took of the religion of his day, as expressed by him in his work on laws, is strictly conservative; the old religion is to be kept and regulated in the interests of the State. The profound religious content of Plato's world of Forms was not perceived until five hundred years after his death, and from then on it left its mark all the more strongly on religious thought. Since then no religion has neglected Plato.

Herodotos, the Father of History, has a passage to this effect:

As to the origin of each of the gods, or whether they all had always been, and what their appearance was, they (the Greeks) had no notion until, one might say, a few days ago. Hesiod and Homer, in my opinion, lived four hundred years before my time, not more, and it is they whose poetry gave the Greeks the genealogy of the gods, their titles, their several ranks and occupations, and made known their outward semblance.

This saying is a forerunner of the rationalism which soon was to teach openly that the gods were human inventions, but there is an element of truth in it.

Homer was not the Bible of the Greeks in the sense that his poems were a holy document, but he had the same power of men's minds that the Bible had in old days when no one dreamed of doubting it. Homer was the first school-book; many knew long passages by heart, some could recite every canto. Homer's description of the gods, what they looked like, how they appeared, what they did, was implanted from the beginning in the Greeks' thought; and as Homer described the gods, the artists saw them. Taken in that way, Herodotos' statement that Homer made the gods is right, though he did not, in the strict sense, do so, for they are far older than Homer. If we include under the name of Homer the conceptions contained in his poems, which go back to the heroic age of the Mycenaean civilization, then he also created the divine commonwealth, with Zeus, the chief god, at its head. Zeus is king, the other gods are his vassals, and there is also a divine proletariat, which on one occasion is summoned to an assembly of the deities. Zeus gathers his vassals about him to take counsel or share a feast in his palace, which stands on the top of the walled royal citadel, Mount Olympos, surrounded by the dwellings of the other gods. His vassals are often self-willed and refractory, seeking to forward their own interests in opposition to the will of the highest god, and so he must at times resort to strong words and threats to compel their obedience.

Homer's authority so firmly implanted the conception of the commonwealth of the gods under the sceptre of Zeus in the thought of the Greeks that it set at naught the political revolution which early abolished kingship, replacing it with aristocracy or democracy. Earth might be republican, but heaven remained a monarchy. Hesiod's attempt to modernize the conception by making the gods elect Zeus king after their victory over the Titans (in Homer he inherits his position by right of seniority) attracted no attention.

(Hesiod arranged the innumerable multitude of deities in a family tree, beginning with the origin of the world; it would not be true to say 'the creation', for in the beginning there was something, namely, Chaos, disorderly primeval matter, and from Chaos sprang the orderly universe which the Greeks called the Kosmos. The evolution was conceived in the only possible way, as a genealogy. From Chaos came forth the Earth, the Underworld, and Eros, the impulse to reproduction, which may be considered as the motive force of the whole development. From Chaos, again, sprang Darkness and Night, which produced the Ether and Day, and Earth bore her own husband, Heaven (Uranos), the Mountains and the Sea, and, with Heaven, Ocean and the Titans. Then follow the families of gods. Indeed, this is the beginning of a cosmological theory, which later developed into natural philosophy, for that long retained mythological names for its principles; in Hesiod these names are already designations of natural elements.)

Homer created the forms in which the great gods lived in the consciousness of the Greek people and in their art and literature, but with a couple of important exceptions. He has little to say of Demeter, the goddess of husbandry, and of Dionysos, the god of religious ecstasy. The Homeric gods were the common property of the Greeks, but even apart from Homer, these gods were worshipped everywhere. Zeus lived on every mountain-top about which the clouds gathered, Artemis and her nymphs might be encountered in field and forest, Demeter's festivals were celebrated wherever Greeks lived. But, universal though these deities were, in cult they were attached to definite places; Athena at Athens was not the same as Athena at Sparta or Thebes. A similar conception is to be found in Catholic countries to-day in the cult of the Madonna and the saints. And here we touch on the question of popular piety. So far we have been speaking of gods, as they lived in the general Hellenic consciousness and were formed in art and literature, especially in Homer; but how did the gods appear in the everyday life of Greece? What was their position in the belief and piety of the people?

(Greece had no professional priesthood; there was no such thing as a priest whose lifework it was to dedicate himself to the service of the gods and to guard their temples and other property. Priests were citizens who, besides their activities in civic life, had the task of seeing to the cult of a god and looking after his temple. Whereas in the East literary activity, tradition and speculation and such beginnings of science as existed were in the hands of the priesthood, all that was, in Greece, the business of laymen, poets and thinkers, from the beginning. The significance of this is immense, for it and it alone was the prerequisite for free thought and for the rise of philosophy and science.)

The origin of this fundamental state of things is perhaps to be found in primeval times, when the father of a family, by reason of his position as head of the house, had likewise to care for its worship, for the relations between the family and the higher powers. Religious practices have from the very beginning been connected with the community and its subdivisions, a connexion which never ceased to exist in the historical period of Greece. Domestic worship formed an important although inconspicuous part. Its central point was the hearth, on which some morsels of food were put at meals, while at the close of the meal a few drops of wine were poured out, ceremonies which were kept up from old habit as unreflectingly as our grace before meat. Numerous domestic altars, dedicated to various gods, have been discovered in excavations. The larder was protected by its own gods, the courtyard by Zeus Herkeios. Outside the door stood the stone pillar of Apollo Agyieus and the triple figure of Hekate, which averted all evil. It is important to notice, as showing the significance of the domestic cult, that when evidence of citizenship was wanted, an Athenian citizen proved his civic rights by referring to his altar of Zeus Herkeios, to Apollo Patroos (i.e. inherited from his fathers), and his ancestral graves. Religion formed a part of everyday life in a way which is far from easy for us to understand.

The cult of the dead, that is of the ancestors, united the living and the departed members of the clan. It was a sacred duty to bring offerings to the tombs, libations and presents of food, although the old idea that these offerings were needed for the dead man's existence in his grave assuredly was fading; but the dead took heavy vengeance for any neglect. Equally binding was the duty of burying a corpse, at least of casting three handfuls of earth on the dead body. Many customs, rites of purification and certain meals, had to be observed in a house of mourning. In the old days, great families celebrated the obsequies of a departed kinsman with lavish display, wherein their pride of race and self-esteem found expression. The oldest Attic vases, dating from the eighth century B.C., show us magnificent funeral processions, with throngs of men and of mourning women. Legislation waged war on such pompous and useless extravagance, forbidding among other things animal sacrifices. Its success in limiting sepulchral luxury, the noblest product of which is the beautiful Athenian grave-monuments, was assuredly due not merely to social developments which overthrew the superior position of the nobility, but also to the dominance of the Homeric conception of the underworld as the abode of lifeless and powerless phantoms. The after-life was nothing, although myths told of enemies of the gods, such as Tantalos and Sisyphos, who were punished in the underworld. The cult at tombs went on in the traditional forms until the end of antiquity.

The family had its own peculiar worships, which were inherited within the kin. Herodotos, for instance, says concerning the statesman Isagoras that his kin worshipped Zeus Karios. As the power of the State increased, it took the more important of these cults to itself, but often allowed the office of priest to remain hereditary in the kin. Thus the hierophant, the chief officiant in the Eleusinian Mysteries, always belonged to the clan of the Eumolpidai, the priestess of Athena Poliás, the city goddess, and the priest of Poseidon-Erechtheus, always to the Eteobutadai; the Buzygai performed the sacred ploughing at the foot of the Akropolis. A family would trace its origin to a hero (Butes and Buzyges, in the case of the last two named), and ultimately to a god. This is important for the effective power of the idea of descent, although it has no religious significance, for a mythological ancestor, an eponym as he was called, could be invented for States and families. When Kleisthenes put through his democratic reforms in Athens, not only in the political but also in the religious sphere, in order to destroy the predominance of the ancient clans, the ten new tribes into which the people were divided received Attic heroes as their fictitious ancestors.

The religion of the State was modelled on that of the family and the clan, which it inherited together with its pretensions, for it put its power more and more in place of the old clan-organization. The religious centre of the State was the State hearth in the council-chamber, from which colonists, going forth to found a new city abroad, used to take fire for their own State hearth. In the most ancient times, the chief guardian of the State worship was the same person who looked after the secular affairs of the community, namely, the king. When kingship was abolished, the king's sacral duties passed to a republican official, but he often, for instance at Athens, bore the title of king, an expression of the conservatism which belongs to the religious sphere. The State, in its democratic popular assemblies, decided all affairs of religious importance, but acknowledged the power of the gods by seeking confirmation from the oracle at Delphoi, for instance in questions of alterations in old cults and the introduction of new ones.

Religious activities guided the lives of the citizens in a much more intensive fashion and on far more frequent occasions than we would suppose. To take instances from Athens, which we are best acquainted with, the new-born child was received into the family by being carried around the hearth some few days after birth. A little later, the phratry (a sort of ecclesiastical community) was notified of the birth, and a sacrifice was then offered, as was done also when a boy's hair was cut, that is to say when he entered upon adolescence, and when a girl was married. Youths and maidens took part in processions, choirs, and certain festivals. When the youth became a man, it was highly likely that he would fill some office of a religious nature, for priesthoods were numerous and were divided up among the citizens, while even secular officials, such as generals, had certain sacrifices to perform. It might be a man's duty to offer some sacrifice, to organize a festival or a procession, or some lesser charge might be entrusted to him on a like occasion.

Greek religion was indissolubly connected with the community and its component parts, State, clan, and family. It cannot be called a State religion in the ordinary meaning of those words, for it was that side of the communal life in which due respects were paid to the gods and their goodwill and grace were assured. Although the religious ceremonial of Greece never reached the same formalism as that of Rome, one might be inclined to describe it as superficial; yet it had its value, not only from the social but from the religious point of view. We may speak of collective piety, like that of Swedish rural communities in old times. The individual counted simply as a link in the chain of the clan, as one citizen of a State; to be cast out from the clan and the State was, next to death, the heaviest punishment which could be inflicted on anyone; such a man had neither home nor rest. The gods who protected the clan and the State protected also their members and showed kindness to them. Everyone was responsible for paying them reverence and must fulfil their demands, for an offence against them was avenged not only on the criminal but on his clan and State. Piety towards the gods bound the members of clan and State together in conscious union in relation to the higher powers. And these duties descended from ancient usage; how often, when religious matters are mentioned, do we meet with that old phrase, 'according to ancestral custom'!

That is the reason for an attitude in religious matters which arouses wonder in a man of later times. Not to fulfil the obligations of cult was an offence which risked forfeiting the gods' grace for the family and also for the community; but everyone might think and say what he chose concerning the gods, for it was not the communal religion, but only poetry and myth which described the gods' appearance and activity. Even within the limits thus fixed, the individual might find satisfaction and be filled with piety towards and reverence for the gods, so long as he recognized that he was a link in the chain of the clan, a citizen of his State. He found his satisfaction in the collective piety within the circle of clansmen and of fellow citizens of the community, and knew that his peace was securely made with the gods.

But, as was remarked a little before, even the great gods generally worshipped had their local attachments in cult, and were connected with the close union of religion and the community. For the gods were the gods of the States, and so Athena at Athens was not the same as Athena at Sparta, indeed the former was sometimes spoken of as 'Athena who rules over Athens'. The clans had long been settled each in a certain place where it had its landed possessions; many Attic communities (the so-called demes) were named after clans. So their gods were also settled. On the other hand, local associations of gods very often depended upon places of worship. We make a spot holy by putting a sanctuary there; but in antiquity, the holiness belonged to the place itself, and a sanctuary was erected there because the spot was holy. Zeus was surnamed after the mountains about whose summits he gathered his clouds, Artemis and other deities often after well-known sanctuaries. In addition, there were the countless swarms of godlings and semi-divine beings who often were worshipped only in a single spot. The Nymphs, who were much worshipped, particularly by women, had their cults in caves and beside springs. River-gods, whose popularity is made plain by the river-names which form part of personal names, as Kephisodotos, 'gift of the river Kephisos', had their places of worship at the river whose name the god bore. Purely topographical also was the penetration of human life by religion in ancient times, to a degree which we can hardly picture aright to ourselves. True, in modern Greece the little chapels in which, at most, Mass is said once a year are amazingly numerous; in some places every family has its chapel. But in ancient Greece the holy places were more numerous still. What Strabo says of the country at the mouth of the river Alpheios is true to some extent of all Greece.

All the region is full of shrines of Artemis, Aphrodite and the Nymphs, in groves full of flowers . . . there are also many shrines of Hermes on the roads and of Poseidon on the sea-shore.

It was hardly possible to take a step outdoors without stumbling on a holy spot, a chapel, a sacred precinct, or at least a herm (pillar with a head of Hermes atop). An ancient writer said with but slight exaggeration that gods were more numerous than human beings.

A very large contribution to this wealth of places of worship was made by the numerous heroes. A hero was properly a dead man, a hero (in our sense) of bygone days, whose worship had overstepped the bounds of his own kin and become general; he was active from his tomb and protected the land in which his remains lay and its people. Heroes aided their own people, and no one else. In the war with the Persians, heroes were seen fighting in the Athenian ranks against the national enemy. Many of them, like Muslim saints in our own day, were physicians, for a physician should be near at hand, and they were dear to the hearts of the people who needed their help. However, the heroes were a miscellaneous collection, for nothing like all such worships arose from the cult of a dead man of valour. The recipients of many minor cults, who were too insignificant to be considered gods, were counted among the heroes. There were nameless heroes and heroines, and it was easy to name such beings out of the legends, especially from the rich treasury of the Troy-saga. Oidipus, for instance, was credited with four different graves. Certain inscriptions which furnish a list of the worships in the rural districts of Attica give us a clear idea of how overwhelmingly many the hero-cults were.

We now pass to the forms of the cult, which may seem, and often were, mere matters of external routine, yet piety and devotion to the gods also found their expression in them. Many must have felt what the pious Plutarch expresses:

No visits delight us more than those to shrines, no occasions are more pleasant than festivals, nothing we do or see is sweeter than our actions and sights before the gods, when we take part in ceremonies or dances, when we are present at sacrifices or initiations. . . . Sacrificial feasts are the most delightful.

A Greek temple, unlike a Christian church, was not a building in which the pious gathered together to offer worship; it was the god's dwelling-place, in which his image stood and his possessions were kept. When we hear of a Greek temple, we think of the great masterpieces of architecture, the Parthenon and others, but at the same time the religious value of these glorious shrines is obscured by secondary considerations. Aristotle was of opinion that the tyrants who erected the first great temples built them to make work for their people. It is certain that these dynasts intended to display not only their reverence for the gods but their own power and glory. Even the Parthenon was put up, as was said in its own day by way of reproach against Perikles, to be a pompous manifestation of the might and splendour of the Athenian Empire. Probably many of the little, inconspicuous and poor shrines were dearer to the hearts of pious people as the old, rude wooden figures of gods were holier than the masterpieces of art. Pheidias' statue of Athena in the Parthenon was a show-piece; the real tutelary goddess of Athens was the old olive-wood image in the 'old temple' (the Erechtheion), which was said to have fallen down from heaven. Like many images of the Madonna in our own day, it was clad in a splendid robe and had rich adornment on it.

Many places of worship had not even a modest chapel; the image of the god, if there was one, stood under the open sky, and there was always a plain altar of rough stone or turf. Trees growing in the sacred precinct were protected and might not be cut down; so a grove, in a land so ill supplied with timber as Greece, was often synonymous with a holy place. The deep, cool verdure, with perhaps a purling spring which arose in the grove, was enough to arouse a feeling of peace and rest and it may be also of the mystical presence of the divinity. The feelings which the pious experienced in such a place were doubtless more profound than those which were aroused when they stood before, or in, a showy temple and admired its artistry.

An altar was never lacking, for animal sacrifice was the central ceremony of Greek religion. On the altar were burned those parts of the victim which fell to the gods' share, and the participants roasted their portions over the fire upon it. In the earlier times, there sometimes was a fire-pit for this purpose inside the shrine, but later the altar always found its place outside the temple, where the worshippers of the god assembled on his festival. The sacrificial feast was in a way a communion, a shared meal, which united

gods and men in a bond whose inviolable sanctity is an outstanding feature of all older culture; the meal was holy, often
the portions of meat might not be taken away from the consecrated place and the same rule applied to the remains of
the sacrifice, the ashes and the bones; the skull of the victim
(*bukránion*) was nailed up in the grove around the temple or
against a wall. The danger of this rite losing all inner meaning was great. As every time that a beast was killed at home
the form was that of a sacrifice, it became nothing but a
form; 'lover of sacrifice' (*philothýtes*) means no more than
'hospitable'. The State indulged in mass-sacrifices in order
to give its citizens, who usually lived very plainly, a feast of
meat and a holiday; accounts preserved on inscriptions show
us what large sums the Athenian democracy spent for that
purpose. As a rule, only one great sacrificial festival took
place every year at each temple. The preparations were
elaborate—a great procession, a sacrifice, choirs which sang
hymns and danced in honour of the god; festival games,
athletic contests, and other spectacles were connected with
certain feasts. At great festivals there grew up a motley
fair which had nothing to do with religion, but satisfied the
social need of mankind to get together, do something, and
generally 'let oneself go'. It recurs at the present day in
similar forms, though now the festival is held in honour of
a Panaghia or a saint. We must not for this reason undervalue
the pious feeling which the festivals of the gods could arouse.
Theognis expresses it in some lines which were composed
under the threatening shadow of Persian aggression.

> Lord Phoibos, 'twas thy hand that raised the wall
> Which rings Alkathoos' fortress strong and tall;
> Be thine the hand which layeth low the boast
> Of this our foe, the haughty Median host.
> So shall thy people, each returning spring,
> Glad hecatombs unto thy temple bring,
> While merry harp and cry of praise conspire
> About thine altar with the festal choir.

Festivals are the most evident manifestation of collective religion, but everyone, when he chose to do so, was free to approach a god with a sacrifice, praise, and prayer. He might bring a victim before a god and offer it together with his family; various reliefs represent family sacrifices of this kind; significantly, most of them are to the physician-god Asklepios. Inside the temple, before the statue of the deity, there generally stood a table, on which anyone who chose to approach the god would lay bloodless offerings, cakes, fruit, and the like. It was not proper for anyone who had a petition to make to a god to come without a gift, and anyone who had been delivered from a danger, recovered from an illness, had had his prayer answered, or had made a profit, expressed his gratitude by a present to the god to whom he ascribed that benefit. In the last-named case the gift was often called a tithe; the common modern term 'votive offering' is of Latin origin and arises from the practice of promising a gift in case a prayer was answered and presenting it when this happened. But it would seem that in Greece this hardly took place in a manner so outspokenly commercial as with the more formal Romans. Most of their gifts were the spontaneous expression of gratitude, as are the ex-votos in Catholic churches of southern Europe in our own times. It is significant that the votive offerings to Athena found on the Akropolis at Athens are very numerous in the times before the Persian War but fall off later and are scarce in the Hellenistic period. This is due, not only to the fact that the remains of the archaic period are better preserved, but also to the decline of piety and to Athena being too important and official for the little man. Small rural temples which the archaeologist's spade seldom touches have yielded a rich harvest of votive offerings, bearing witness to the piety of the local population.

If there was no temple, the gifts were hung up on branches of the trees in the sacred grove. Large votive offerings, statues and the like, were erected in the sacred precinct in front of the temple, while lesser ones were heaped up inside it, so that a much-visited shrine must have given the impression of a cross between a museum and a lumber-room. A metal object would get damaged and broken, but, as it might not be removed, it would be melted down and made into something else, which remained the god's property. The humble gifts of small people, little terra-cotta statuettes, pottery vessels, lamps, and such-like, accumulated in great quantities and were spoiled; now and then a clearance of them had to be made, but they must not leave the sacred precinct but were buried in a pit within it, a welcome storehouse for archaeologists. The abundance of such gifts bears unimpeachable witness to the piety of the people, their trust in and gratitude towards the gods. Mingled with gratitude were other motives, for votive offerings could also serve for display and ostentation. Such a motive can perhaps be seen even in the statues and other works of art erected by individuals, and appears early in the many-figured groups which various cities dedicated at Delphoi; at the beginning of the Sacred Way stood what may reasonably be called an Avenue of Victory, preserving the memory of the Greeks' triumphs over one another. There, and also at Olympia, the lesser gifts became so numerous that there was no room for them in the temple, and many States erected treasuries, as they are called, to preserve them in.

He who approached the gods to offer them a sacrifice, present a petition, or merely visit their holy place must be free from all pollution, ritually pure. At the beginning of the sacrifice a brand was taken from the altar, dipped in water, and the sacrificer and victim sprinkled with it. At the entrance to the temple stood a vessel of water, with which the visitor asperged himself before going in. There were many occasions in daily life which caused pollution, such as visiting a house where there was a corpse, being near a woman in childbirth, and so forth, but the worst defilement that could be incurred was by shedding human blood. The pollution was washed off with water, like dirt. If a more thorough purification was needed, a sucking-pig was sacrificed and its blood used for cleansing; this was done in purifying from blood-guilt and before every meeting of the popular Assembly at Athens. In certain cults, particularly mysteries, and in the case of many priests, stricter rules were in force, but the Greeks kept their precepts concerning purity within reasonable bounds and did not develop them, despite certain tendencies that way to which we shall come later, into a ceremonial law which governed the whole of life. On the contrary, the ritual requirement of purity became the starting-point of ethical precepts. This was true above all of blood-pollution, of which something will be said later on. That purity of heart is the principal demand is eloquently expressed in a Hellenistic epigram:

> Pure be his soul who enters this pure place
> And here his hand in lustral water laves.
> The good a drop will cleanse, but for the base
> Ocean suffices not with all his waves.

The art of divination formed an important part of religion, and had a profound influence on men's everyday and social life. The willingness of the gods to throw a light on future events by means of signs was fully believed in, and the ancients never doubted the possibility of foreseeing the future by means of signs, or of dreams, which also are sent by the gods. By certain signs in a victim it could be made out if it was acceptable to the gods, and therefore sacrifices were performed before important undertakings, especially in war, so as to be informed of the outcome. Omens were taken from the flight and cries of birds, from the fall of lots, from things accidentally heard, and so forth. To explain an omen or interpret a presage needed special skill, which was the possession of professional interpreters of signs, and of seers.

Much is said of the oracles which were connected with the holy places of certain gods. Herodotos' reports testify to their flourishing condition at the time of the Persian War;

later many of them ceased, being overcome partly by the growing doubts as to their reliability, partly by popular and more convenient methods of getting oracles. The oracles' advice was asked about all kinds of petty matters of daily life, and also concerning weighty decisions in public affairs and in war, but above all, in things of religious significance the will of the gods must be discovered. Foremost of all the oracles in importance and prestige was that of Apollo at Delphoi. Here his priestess, the Pythia, gave ecstatic prophecies from the tripod, but his clever priests turned the words she uttered into verse and assuredly gave them not form only, but also content. The Delphic oracle is very old and probably was to begin with much like any other, but thanks to skilful exploitation of the possibilities furnished by requests for its advice, it gained a unique authority in all affairs religious and political during the archaic period. Beyond a doubt, much experience was stored up by the able priesthood, so that they could give good advice. The Delphic Apollo canonized heroes, gave his sanction to cults and their ordinances, enjoined rules for purity and purifica- tions, added a certain amount of moral precepts, encouraged the development of a regular calendar, and supported the laws of States with his authority. Finally we may recollect the numerous oracles which passed from mouth to mouth and usually were ascribed to mythical prophets, of whom the most famous were Bakis and the Sibyl; these were often employed as a powerful weapon in the service of political propaganda.

In time the Delphic oracle, like all the rest, lost much of its authority. The decline was due in no small measure to the Greeks' loss of political independence, but was connected also with the growth of a critical spirit. As long as the old belief was alive, the Greeks did not lack divine guidance in all the chances and changes of life, any more than they lacked an authority in religious concerns. As already said, divination (*mantikē*) was an important part of religion, exercising a continual influence on life, whether private, public, or religious.

A concrete example gives a livelier picture than a general description. Let us present ourselves at Athena's temple on the Akropolis of Athens in the sixth century B.C., before the Persians ruined and burned the citadel; posterity has their destruction to thank for it that it knows the Akropolis of that day so well, for in levelling the ground for the glorious new buildings of the fifth century, the Parthenon and the Erechtheion, the ruined remains were thrown indiscriminately in to fill up. The Akropolis was the citadel of Athens, the last refuge in the extremities of war, and in older times still it was the city. Human dwellings were not yet cleared off it; among them rose the temple of Athena, which was built on the ruins of the Mycenaean prince's palace and is usually called Solon's, because it was erected in his old age. The pediments were decorated with brightly painted figures in limestone. In that temple stood the old wooden image of Athena, which on a certain day every year was stripped of its clothing and ornaments and taken to the nearest shore to be bathed in the sea. Peisistratos rebuilt the temple handsomely and provided it with new pedimental sculptures in marble, Athena's battle with the Giants. Near by were the mark of Poseidon's trident, a salt spring, and the tomb of the legendary king of Athens, Kekrops, all of which were incorporated in the Erechtheion, along with Athena's olive-tree, which was burned by the Persians but immediately put forth a green branch a yard long. In the temple lived Athena's serpent, her house-snake, which quitted its quarters as the Persians approached, for which reason the Athenians readily evacuated their city and gave it over to the enemy. In the warm spring evenings was heard the melodious cry of the little owls which had their nests in the crannies of the rocks. The owl was Athena's bird, which, at the battle of Marathon, was seen flying among the ranks of the fighters. Under the north wall of the citadel a stair led down; at a certain festival two young girls, who lived near the temple, received from the priestess of Athena mysterious holy objects which they carried down this stair to a sanctuary in the city, and brought others back from it. The priestess belonged to the ancient noble family of the Eteobutadai. At the height of summer, a great sacrificial procession moved up to the temple. Probably it carried even then a new mantle for Athena, woven by Athenian virgins in the service of the goddess, for that mantle was carried as the sail of a ship on wheels at the Great Panathenaia, held every four years, a development of the old festival introduced by Peisistratos. All around the temple were placed votive offerings, statues of men, horsemen, and young women in the most elegant costume of the day. These last are so numerous that they now fill a whole room in the little museum on the Akropolis; perhaps they were priestesses, or they may have had their statues consecrated for some other reason. The inscriptions on the pedestals testify to piety, but also to the desire to get something for being pious. The interior of the temple must have been full of votive offerings. Metal objects are scarce; doubtless they were plundered or removed. But fragments of the beautiful Athenian pottery and vase-paintings of that time are so numerous that the reproductions of them fill a work in many volumes.

Ancient ritual observances and primeval memorials of cult were fitted into a framework which grew steadily more beautiful as the importance of the State increased. Athena protected Athens, and the Athenians showed gratitude and piety to her.

The object of these introductory lines has been to give a general view of the older, national Greek religion in its most universal form. Many peculiar ceremonial customs and many cults, often confined to one locality although of great interest for religion and for the history of religion (e.g. the Eleusinian Mysteries), could find no place in an exposition which aimed only at what holds good generally.

The reader will perhaps object that this review concerns itself too much with outward forms and does not describe the spirit which made those forms live. Such an objection is but partly justified. The costume which Greek religion wore was not sewn nor fitted by indifferent hands, but is rather to be compared with the covering which Nature puts upon living creatures. The forms of Greek religion are the organic outgrowth of its essence, and therefore also an expression of it; priestly speculation is wanting. The form of this religion gives the background to the religious feeling which grew up within that framework, and a knowledge of this background is an indispensable prerequisite for our principal object, to which we now pass, a description of religious feeling in Greece.

I

RELIGION IN THE ARCHAIC PERIOD

I. ECSTATIC AND MYSTIC MOVEMENTS

NO religion has ever been so consistently anthropo-morphic as that of Greece. Its gods were like human beings both outwardly and inwardly, the mysterious power which gods have in most religions was reduced as much as possible, and an attempt was made to explain their activities and interventions in a fashion comprehensible to the ordinary intelligence. It has been said that in Homer there are three classes of human beings, the common people, the nobles, and the gods. This would be correct if the gods were not immortal. A sharp distinction is made between gods and men, and to try to overstep it is *hybris*, frowardness, going too far, any such attempt being severely punished, as Thersites is chastised for daring to speak against his lords. In the mother country the feeling concerning the gods and their power was more naïve, but art soon represented them in the familiar form, and as art and poetry portrayed them, so they appeared in the eyes of the people.

In such a religion there is a gulf fixed between gods and men, but no place for a deep inward longing to overleap that gulf, to know that deity is near, to be united with it, to be absorbed in it, in short for a mystical feeling in religion which may find expression in silent aspiration, pious contemplation, or dizzy ecstasy.

(Greek religion was from the beginning connected with a society, whether family, clan, or State. A man did not choose his gods, but was born to them; clan and State gave him his deities and his religion. Under such circumstances, col-lective piety can arise, but for the individual the possibility of satisfying his personal religious needs or giving expression to his deeper religious strivings is narrowly limited. The community has a tight hold on him.)

It has been conjectured that the religion of the pre-Hellenic population contained a certain ecstatic tendency which came to light in the worship of vegetation-deities, the connexion of which with life and death is obvious, and that this was suppressed by the more sober religion of the invading Greeks. Be this as it may, at the beginning of the historic period religious ecstasy emerged with irresistible force. Or, to speak more correctly, it was shortly before the light of history begins to shine upon Greece, for our information concerning the emergence of the Dionysiac ecstasy is in the form of myths, which poets reshaped into their familiar descriptions of the god's irresistible and consuming might. The movement seems especially to have taken possession of the women, who are more inclined than men to an emotional religion and more easily got hold of by one.

In a general way, the Dionysiac ecstasy is described as follows. Women are seized by a mental disturbance, sometimes despite resistance at first; they abandon their occupations, hurry out into the woods and fields, and wander about among the mountains, dancing and waving torches and thyrsi, the latter being sticks wound with ivy and having a pine-cone at the end. Milk and honey spring up from the ground; we seldom hear of wine. The god Dionysos in person reveals himself. As the ecstasy reaches its climax, the maenads, as they are called, seize a beast, tear it in pieces, and devour bits of its flesh raw. Those who resist or try to hinder the ecstasy are severely dealt with.

That a reality lies behind these descriptions of a barbaric rite, a savage ecstasy, cannot be denied and is proved by certain survivals of later date. In Plutarch's day, the maenads still wandered about on the snow-clad peaks of Parnassos; but these maenads were no throngs of women seized by ecstasy, spirit-summoned, but Delphic and Athenian religious colleges. A sacrifice of raw meat is mentioned as late as Hellenistic times in a regulation for cult. The primitive rite is usually considered as a communion. The beast which the maenads tore in pieces is the god himself, and they take him and his power into themselves by swallowing the bleeding morsels. Even if this was the original significance of the rite, it is far from certain that Dionysos' worshippers in Greece were conscious of it. It is sufficient to suppose that the Dionysiac orgies are a result of the tendency towards ecstasy and its violent expression which exists in the depths of many persons' souls and now and then, for reasons unknown, breaks out and spreads with wild speed, for it is infectious, a fact which plainly appears in myths concerning the Dionysiac orgies. It reminds us of the epidemics of dancing in the Middle Ages and similar phenomena in more recent times.

It would seem that the Dionysiac orgies swept over Greece like a river in flood, but they met a counter-current strong enough to dam them and lead them into ordinary and quieter channels of Greek religion. This was legalism under the auspices of Apollo of Delphoi, of which we shall soon have more to say. Apollo was clever enough to realize that so strong a movement could not be suppressed; he therefore took it up and fitted it to the forms of Greek cult. He set Dionysos beside himself at Delphoi and pruned his worship of what was dangerous in it by giving it a place in State cult. This brought with it abundant and peculiar motive forces; we need only remind ourselves that dramatic performances were a part of the worship of Dionysos.

The condition of our sources prevents us from giving an opinion as to whether the Dionysiac ecstasy was anything more than an elemental outburst of religious excitement or brought with it certain religious ideas. There is no sufficient reason for recognizing in this movement the concepts of death and resurrection which appear in the cult of Dionysos in later times. On the other hand, this movement put out a branch which from the religious point of view is very remarkable, Orphism. While our older documents concerning Orphism are scarce and disputable, still they give us some notion of the new and revolutionary ideas which it brought into the religious life of Greece. Orphism must not be treated by itself; it was the main trunk of the powerful and wide-spreading religious growths which in the earlier times sprang up as a protest against the narrow ancestral collective piety, and are so closely connected with Orphism that it is neither possible nor justifiable to make a separation.

Orphism is named after Orpheus. He is a mythical figure, famous as a singer, whose renown depends in fact upon the poem which passed under his name; Orphism has not unjustly been called a book-religion. Its god was Dionysos, who in that form was later called Zagreus also. According to the existing myth (although this is not found until the later tradition) we are told that Zeus meant to hand over the sovranty of the universe to his son Dionysos, but the wicked Titans enticed the child to them, tore him in pieces, and devoured his limbs. Athena rescued the heart and brought it to Zeus, and from it the younger Dionysos was created. Zeus smote the Titans with his lightning and burned them to ashes, and from these mankind arose. Orphism had also a cosmogony, which, while to a great extent dependent on Hesiod, introduced a new theme, which yet was very old, for it is to be found among many peoples of the older stages of culture. The world was hatched from an egg. From this egg came forth the first god, Eros, who was later named Phanes and said to be bisexual.

The relation of Orphism to Dionysos is peculiar. The mythic prophet Orpheus died by being torn to pieces by Thracian maenads, a myth which bears witness to an opposition between Orphism and the Dionysiac orgies, which, however, is not hard to understand. For Orphism transformed the outstanding rite of the orgies, the tearing in pieces of a beast (or even a human being, in the myths) and the devouring of its limbs, into the original sin, the Titans' tearing in pieces and devouring of the child Dionysos. This opposition may be compared in some sort to that between

Judaism and Christianity, which appropriated the Jewish scriptures and expounded them in a way which seemed sheer blasphemy to the Jews.

The myth concerning the origin of man is much more important than that concerning the creation of the world. Plato alludes to it when he says that anyone who will not obey his rulers, his elders, and the gods 'displays the so-called ancient Titanic nature'. This Titanic nature is man's evil inheritance, but he has in him also a spark of the divine, a portion of Dionysos. In another passage Plato mentions the doctrine that the body is the tomb of the soul, in which it lies buried during life, and adds that the Orphics call it so because the soul is shut up in the body as in a prison till it has made satisfaction for its sins. The soul is the divine part of man, the body its prison. The Homeric conception of the living body as the man himself and the soul as a pale, lifeless shadow is completely inverted. How this total inversion was possible we can understand from a passage in Pindar. The body, he says, follows mighty death, but the soul abides, which alone comes from the gods. The soul, he continues, sleeps while the limbs are busy, but when men sleep it shows the future in dreams. The meaning is that, as dreams are sent by the gods and the soul is divine, the soul must be free from the confinement of the body to experience the divine, that is, dreams. A similar view is met with again in the stories of extraordinary men whose soul soared free while the body lay in a trance; we shall have more to say of this later on.

With this complete inversion of soul and body in their mutual relations and value is connected an Orphic trait which particularly attracted contemporary notice, their ascetic mode of life. They were vegetarians and considered it unlawful to kill a beast, a thing which must have aroused attention and caused scandal, seeing that animal sacrifice and the sacrificial meal were the most characteristic and universal ceremony of Greek religion. Probably the reason for this prohibition is to be found in the doctrine of transmigration of souls, although this is not ascribed in so many words to the Orphics, but Pindar, who was deeply influenced by the Orphic movement, knows of it. In one place he says that after nine years Persephone sends up to the sunlight those who have paid the penalty for her ancient grief, and that from them there arise glorious kings and men great in power and wisdom. Another and obscure passage is to be understood to mean that souls which commit sin in the other world are sent back to this world to be punished, exactly as sins committed here are punished in the underworld. In the other world, the good live in bliss, while the wicked endure a punishment 'which none can look upon'. But those who have kept their hearts from unrighteousness during three residences in both the upper and lower worlds go by the Road of Zeus, past the Tower of Kronos, to the Islands of the Blessed. The transmigration comes to an end. This life is wholly parallel with the other; the soul lives in both alternately, it can commit an offence in both and be punished in both. Against this background we can better understand Euripides' question whether life be not a death and death a life, a question to which Plato gives his approbation. An inversion of this life and the other took place, and thus we can explain the paradox that the body is the grave of the soul. As the soul is freed when the body dies, and goes into the other world, so it is confined in the prison of the body when it is sent up into this world again.

The Orphics laid much stress on purifications from guilt and pollution, a thing which is particularly noticeable in the period before the Persian War, during which famous priestly specialists in purification were active. As later on the exaggerated anxiety about pollution lessened, it was the Orphics who became most concerned with purifications. They wandered about the country inviting individuals and States to free themselves, by means of purificatory rites, from guilt and punishment. Doubtless there were charlatans among these priestly purifiers, who helped to arouse the contempt with which Orphism was treated in Plato's day, but Orphism was in deadly earnest with its desire for purity, of which the purifications were the ritual expression, and the desire was based upon the pessimistic view it took of human nature and its need not only of outward but of moral purity. Like all religious zealots, the Orphics were persuaded that they and no others were in the right. They shared the contemporary opinion that punishment was retribution, of which we shall have more to say later. Punishment will overtake a man for his errors and offences, and if it does not fall upon the wrongdoer in this life, it awaits him in the next. Thus the conceptions of the other life and the underworld underwent a fateful alteration. Alongside the Homeric, indeed the general Greek, concept of the realm of lifeless, unconscious shadows was that of a place of punishment and on the other hand of the blessed region of the pious, which had its prototype in Elysion, described already in Homer, but to which he represents only chosen favourites of the gods as being admitted. Now Elysion became the dwelling-place of the pious and the underworld that of the wicked, but more was said of the place of punishment than of Elysion.

He who was not purified from his pollution was to 'lie in filth' in the underworld, one example of the very common idea that the other life is a continuation of this one and that such a continuation beyond death was in itself a punishment. The pains and penalties of the underworld were further painted in lively colours, which borrowed from myths of the punishments of enemies of the gods and from earthly punishments; in this connexion the idea appears that the manner of the punishment will correspond to the kind of wrongdoing, a sort of *ius talionis*. A famous example of these fancies is the picture of the underworld with which the great painter Polygnotos, not long after the war against Persia, decorated the Lounge of the Knidians at Delphoi. There, among other things, were to be seen a patricide being strangled by his father, one guilty of sacrilege tortured with poison and other things, and a demon named Eurynomos, sitting on the skin of a vulture, half-black and half-blue like a meat-fly, showing his teeth in a grimace, and eating the flesh off the bones of the dead. Thus arose a new conception, which produced fateful and very long-lasting after-effects: belief in a place of punishment. Alongside it stood the common belief in the bloodless shadow-realm of Hades; the belief in a Hell grew dim in classical times which welcomed life, but it left an aftergrowth which made many uneasy. A later age developed it further and in yet stronger colours and proved what a terrible power it could have over human feelings.

The doctrine of retribution may have been sufficient for some, but probably the Orphics, like the Pythagoreans, united with it the theory of transmigration of souls, which we found in the poem of Pindar just quoted. The circle of births is not everlasting but has an end, for the righteous man is justified and makes his way to eternal bliss. Probably Pindar's pronouncement is a combination of the doctrine of transmigration with the old myth of Elysion, the Fields of the Blessed, but this does not lessen the fullness and depth of his thought. Such a doctrine is the natural consummation of Orphism; the ultimate liberation of mankind from its Titanic inheritance. Therein lay the higher meaning of the purifications and asceticism to which the Orphics, like the Pythagoreans, subjected themselves. Such a way of life was not for everyone. Orphism was bound to remain a sect, and it was still more the case that this imperishable religious idea, clad as it was in a grotesque disguise, could be understood only by the loftiest spirits, by a Pindar or a Plato.

The ideas with which we have just been concerned were not the peculiar property of the Orphics but belonged to a wider movement of which Orphism was the most conspicuous expression. Its originality and the wide scope of its conceptions cannot be understood except against the background of the other movements which obscured and overcame it, but have also certain traits in common with it; we will shortly proceed to a detailed exposition of them. By way of a general account of the importance of Orphism I cannot do better than repeat the words I used in my book on the history of Greek religion.

Orphism is the combination and crown of all the restless and manifold religious movements of the archaic period. The development of the cosmogony in a speculative direction, with the addition of an anthropogony which laid the principal emphasis on the explanation of the mixture of good and evil in human nature; the legalism of ritual and life; the mysticism of cult and doctrine; the development of the other life into concrete visibility, and the transformation of the lower world into a place of punishment by the adaptation of the demand for retribution to the old idea that the hereafter is a repetition of the present; the belief in the happier lot of the purified and the initiated;—for all these things parallels, or at least suggestions, can be found in other quarters. The greatness of Orphism lies in having combined all this into a system, and in the incontestable originality which made the individual in his relationship to guilt and retribution the centre of its teaching. But from the beginning Orphism represented itself as the religion of the elect; others were repelled by the fantastic and grotesque mythological disguise in which it clothed its thoughts. The age took another direction; the demand of the Greek mind for clarity and plastic beauty carried the day. In the clear and rarified atmosphere of the period of great national exaltation which followed the victory over the Persians the mists and the figures of cloud were dissipated. Orphism sank to the level of the populace, but it persisted there until Time once more wrought a transformation and the overlordship of the Greek spirit was broken after more than half a millennium. Then Orphism raised its head again, and became an important factor in the new religious crisis, the last of the ancient world.

To throw further light on certain sides of the religious temper of the archaic period we may add a few words concerning the remarkable men who were active at that time and bear an undeniable resemblance to the shamans of primitive peoples. The souls of two of them, Epimenides and Hermotimos, are said to have been able to quit their bodies and wander about by themselves, during which time they saw many things which were said and done in distant places. Aristeas of Prokonnesos fell dead, his body disappeared, but a traveller met and talked with him a long way off. Seven years later he returned and composed a poem about the Arimaspians, a fabulous people. He revealed himself again at Metapontum and said that he had gone before Apollo in the shape of a raven. Of Abaris the story is told that he carried Apollo's arrow, or rode on it, around the world without taking any food. All these men, except Hermotimos, of whom we have not much information, came forward as priests dealing in purificatory rites—Epimenides' activities at Athens are the best known—and they wrote poems in which they doubtless expressed their religious views. They lived, at latest, in the middle of the sixth century B.C., and afterwards were no longer to be found in Greece, but in Sicily a hundred years later a man was working who gained a place among philosophers, but at the same time belonged to the same sort of people as those just mentioned. This was Empedokles. He was a wonder-worker, the author of a poem with the significant title *Purifications*, a teacher of the doctrine of transmigration who forbade the killing of beasts. He was conscious of his own divinity, for he says:

In me you see a deathless god and no longer a mortal; I go my way honoured among all, as is my due, with fillets and fresh garlands hung about me. When I enter a city, folk past counting follow me to ask for the path that leads to their profit.

Concerning the end of his life marvellous tales were in circulation. Erwin Rohde is right when he says that Empedokles, when the times had already changed greatly, is the last brilliant figure to be included in the series of prophets, priestly purifiers, and miracle-workers, the rest of whom were active in the sixth century B.C.

In the centuries preceding the Persian War, Greece presented a picture very unlike our usual conceptions of the Hellenic world. Maenads in their ecstasy raged in the woods and fields, Orphics preached that man's sinful nature must be subdued and purified by mortifications to avoid punishment in the other world. The land was full of prophets, wandering seers, collectors of oracles, Bakis, the Sibyl and their like, workers of miracles, and purifying priests. Some composed poems about the origin of the world and of the gods, some took no nourishment, some could send their souls wandering free from their bodies. They were called upon to perform purifications and atonements. By expiations and purifications plagues and epidemics were averted, contagious religious frenzies among hysterical women were conjured, lawless and treacherous bloodshed in political strife was cleansed, and rest and relaxation brought, at least for the moment, to fevered minds.

In the religious movements of that age individual needs bore fruit; the need for peace with the gods produced legalism, the need for union with them, mysticism; the desire for retribution for evil deeds gave rise to the conception of the underworld as a place of punishment. Mankind strove to break the confining bonds of collective religion and sought a religion which could give more profound satisfaction to its spiritual needs. These impulses, which were directed to the individual, knew no State boundaries and involved a protest against the particularist religion which had its roots in communal life; a battle was, at least unconsciously, fought out between the religion of humanity in general and of the individual and the official and particularist religion. That age seethed with religious unrest, with new impulses and new ideas. What was it to bring forth for the future?

2. LEGALISM

Competing with the ecstatic and mystic religious feelings above described there appeared from the beginning of the archaic period the legalistic, of which to some extent there are traces in the former tendencies also. Legalism is the attempt to win the grace and favour of the gods by fulfilling

their commandments. In some religions, as those of Judaea
and Persia, legalism developed into a ritual law, whose commands and prohibitions are binding on human life down to
minute details. The sound good sense of the Greeks kept
them from going to any such extreme, but they went part
of the way.

Legalism confronts us in the earliest Greek poem whose
author shows any personal and individual features, Hesiod's
Works and Days. Hesiod has commands which bear witness
to a piety which penetrated the whole of life. The command
that before setting hand to the plough to begin work on the
land, prayer should be offered to Zeus and Demeter that the
crops may produce heavy and full ears, is a consecration of
work which reminds us of Protestant piety. In piety and
purity sacrifice is to be offered to the gods according to one's
means, libation poured and incense burned to them on
going to bed and at daybreak. With these commands are
associated others which bear the stamp of ritualism. A river
is not to be forded without looking towards the water, pray-
ing and washing one's hands, for the gods are wroth with any
who pass over a stream without cleansing their hands and
washing away their evil. Food is not to be taken nor water
ladled out from a vessel which has not been consecrated.
Libations are not to be poured to Zeus with unwashen hands;
one must not urinate in face of the sun nor along a road, nor
uncover one's private parts by the hearth, nor beget a child
after coming back from a funeral, but do so after returning
from a sacrificial feast. Other commands are manifestly
popular rules such as we class among superstitions. The nails
are not to be cut at the time of a sacrificial meal; the ladle is
not to be laid across the bowl from which the wine is drawn;
a man must not bathe in a bath intended for women's use.

Some of the commands recur among the Pythagoreans
in the collection known as the *Symbola Pythagorea*, which,
although there are later additions, goes back to an earlier
period. Among the Pythagorean precepts are a very great

number which are derived from popular belief. A yoke or a broom must not be stepped over; the edge of a knife must be turned away; a loaf should not be broken, nor the fire stirred with a sword, nor bits which fall from the dining-table picked up; one should not turn back when starting on a journey. Some of these are known also from later folk-belief, a few are even now not forgotten. For the Pythagoreans these commands had a deeper meaning and were associated with moral rules. One must not turn aside to visit a shrine, for the gods are not to be treated as a side-issue; a woman is not to be wronged; the best advice is to be given. A later author mentions a command to curb the tongue, and a maxim that it is better to suffer than to do wrong. The Pythagorean precepts are a continuation and development of Hesiod's, and connected with the precepts of the Delphic oracle. They emphasize the demand for purity, and enjoin earnest and genuine reverence for the gods as an indispensable duty. The Pythagoreans' religion used ritual for its foundation, and therefore could include popular rules. They believed in immortality, punishment in the underworld, and transmigration of souls. The arithmetical mysticism which was their peculiar and characteristic feature became important later in theosophy.

The Pythagoreans were the foremost representatives of legalism in ancient Greece, for they really did order their lives according to these numerous and strict rules. There is a supplement to Hesiod's *Works and Days* which, however, is not much later than the poem itself; it shows how far it was possible to go in imposing a set of rules on the business of life. It is the last section and deals with the days of the month—a list of lucky and unlucky days which, revised with the help of astrology, was long authoritative. The first, last, fourth, and seventh days are holy, but the fifth is to be avoided; the sixteenth is not good for plants, but it is for men; it is not lucky for a girl either to be born on that day or to be married; and so on. One or two days are connected

with deities; the seventh is Apollo's birthday, and on the
fifth Horkos, the god who guards oaths, was brought into
the world by the aid of the Erinyes.

It may possibly be thought that all this is popular superstition which has nothing much to do with religion. Be this
as it may, it shows one side of Greek religious sentiment which
must not be neglected, and it is manifest that it has strong
popular roots. In Hesiod, these rules are well on the way to
becoming general precepts for religious purity, handwash-
ings, regulations for sexual conduct and for the bodily
necessities, and so on. To produce a ritual law, the only
thing wanting was that the regulations should be made into
a system and represented as divine ordinances; but the
Greek gods did their people the service of not troubling
themselves about the minutiae of daily life, if only the ceremonial demands of cult were satisfied. Still, the possibility
of confining the whole of human life within the bond of a
ritual law was after all not far distant. The Pythagoreans
accomplished it, but they were only a sect which kept itself
apart from other people and looked down on them. It is of
more importance that this popular legalism formed the background for the activity of the Delphic oracle, which shall
shortly be discussed more fully.

3. JUSTICE

The legalism which has been described above had its
deepest roots in the desire for justice, for rendering unto the
gods what was the gods'. The problem of justice is the red
thread which runs through the contests of the archaic age,
but the battles for justice were fought on the social, not the
religious, plane. Hesiod, the oldest poet of Greece, is a
prophet of justice. He was a peasant, living in poor circumstances in a wretched village in Boiotia; he followed the
profession of a bard and had learned the Homeric form of
speech, but in content his poems are as far removed from
Homer as the east is from the west. Taught by bitter

experience, Hesiod became the herald of justice. In a dispute between him and his brother Perses over their inheritance, the latter tried by means of bribes to induce the high-born judges to give a decision in his favour. In the first part of his poem, the *Works and Days*, Hesiod addresses Perses and advises him to practise justice and get himself wealth by hard work and economy; he addresses the judges, reminding them that the gods are close to mankind and observe those who give crooked verdicts. Zeus has given man justice, which is his patent of nobility, so that he shall not live like the wild beasts who devour one another, because there is no justice among them save the right of the stronger. So the hawk said to the nightingale which it was holding in its sharp talons:

> Fool, spare thy speech! A stronger hath thee fast.
> For all thy song, thou goest where I will,
> To be my meal, or live, if I shall choose.

Hesiod is also the prophet of work. Work gives the just man possession of a livelihood and of property, and justice allows man to enjoy the fruits of his labour. Hesiod's view of life is profoundly pessimistic, for he sees how violence and injustice bear sway. His poetry includes a myth of the ages of the world, which get steadily worse. We live in the Iron Ages, he says in conclusion, and I would I had not been born at this time, for right sits on the end of the spear-shaft and malefactors and violent men are in high places. Men care no more for the gods and no longer revere their aged parents.

Hesiod has been compared to the first great Hebrew prophet, Amos the herdsman of Tekoa, who was his contemporary. Both quiver with a passion for justice, but there is a great difference between their expressions of it. Hesiod's Zeus is not Amos' Yahweh, the jealous god whose very nature is justice and whose wrath smites and punishes the unjust. Zeus had long been, and still is in Hesiod, the champion of justice; his eyes see everything and notice everything; he

fixes a penalty for the haughty who commit wickedness and
shameful deeds, but since Zeus sat enthroned in the far
distance, the result is that his intervention lacks the force
and obviousness which characterize that of Amos' Yahweh.
He sends out watchers who move invisibly about the earth
and observe the doings of mankind. When anyone commits
injustice, Zeus' daughter Dike, the goddess of justice, sits
beside him and complains of the unrighteousness of men,
and when they are oppressed by false dooms, she comes after,
weeping for the evil doings of men who wrong her. To Amos
justice is the very kernel of divine activity, to Hesiod it is
the foundation on which human society rests, given and protected by Zeus. For Amos, justice belongs to the sphere of
deity, for Hesiod, to the human sphere, although it is under
divine protection.

What, then, is justice? We may neglect the philosophic
discussions as to the abstract idea of it, for they came out to
no result; the only important thing for us to know is what
the Greeks themselves thought of it, what denotation the
word *dike* and its cognates had for them. The answer can
be given in one word. For the Greeks, justice was the
retribution which counters wrongdoing. The word *dike*
occurs in such phrases as *diken didónai*, *diken tinein*, literally
to give, to pay, justice, which signify 'to be punished'.
The word *tisis* means 'payment', 'compensation', but also
'revenge', for justice and revenge are not very different,
indeed they coincide when vengeance is taken for wrongdoing. A product of this kind of justice is the *ius talionis*
which was usual in early times and finds pregnant expression in the saying 'an eye for an eye and a tooth for a
tooth'. This is to be traced among the Greeks also; for them,
justice is retributive justice. The Pythagoreans defined
justice as *to antipeponthós*, not an easy phrase to translate:
it signifies 'that which one undergoes in return for something'. This view was so deep-rooted that it now and
then comes out in the older philosophers when they are

describing the course of Nature. Anaximandros of Miletos said:

The boundless is the origin of all that is. It is the law of necessity that things should perish and go back to their origin. For they give satisfaction and pay the penalty (*didónai diken kai tisin*) to one another for their injustice (*adikía*) according to the ordinance of Time.

Aeschylus developed the thought of retributive and punitive justice in more powerful language than anyone else.

> Ye Fates, by God's grace, whither Righteousness leads
> Let the matter determine.
> For Justice, exacting her debt, crieth loud,
> 'For a hateful word, let a word of hate
> Be paid, a blow for a wrathful blow.'
> And old, very old, the command,. 'As ye do,
> Unto you be it done.'

His utterance gains especially in force from the fact that a conviction of divine justice lies at the very root of his religious belief.

In the archaic period, when the power of the State was feeble and undeveloped, justice was obtained by taking the law into one's own hands. The executive had to begin with no means of enforcement at all and later only insufficient ones. In Attic law, distraint was allowable; anyone wishing to enforce payment of a debt after sentence of a court did his own distraining. In the important case of murder or homicide, the power of the State had done away with private action and enforced its right to condemn and punish, but at an earlier period the injured party took the task of punishing into his own hands. Blood-revenge was a sacred duty incumbent upon the survivors, and so unavoidable that the Delphic god laid upon Orestes the obligation of killing his own mother, because she had murdered his father, a tragic conflict which furnishes the material for Aeschylus' masterpiece, the Orestes-trilogy. Only with blood can blood be washed away, and one homicide leads up to another. But

vendettas, whole series of killings, are not found among the
Greeks; the killer underwent the penalty of going into exile,
or, if the kinsmen of the slain were disposed to be merciful,
by paying wergeld. The binding claim of blood-revenge is
given expression in the idea of hereditary guilt, put by
Aeschylus in an arresting form and set up by him in opposition to the belief in the instability of fortune which was
current in his day; we shall have more to say about this later.

> From bygone times men have told the ancient tale
> Of human prosperity,
> How, when waxed great,
> It dies not childless, but hath issue, and
> Born of the luck that blessed the house
> Sorrow cometh, that knows not measure.
> But, alone though I be found, yet
> Otherwise tend my thoughts. Sin
> Is the dam still of a new sin,
> Of a brood like to its parent.
> Let the house cleave to the right,
> Fair is its fortune ever.
>
> For Frowardness, waxing old,
> Beareth new Frowardness,
> Wanton to the bane of men,
> Or soon or late, as the appointed time of birth
> Cometh. A brother hath the child,
> Invincible, unholy, named
> Boldness; and black ruin their coming brings,
> True to the stock that bare them.
>
> But Justice shines bright and clear,
> Though in smoky dwellings,
> Honouring the righteous man.
> But cloth of gold on him whose hands are foul
> She turns her eyes from, rather to seek
> Honesty's house. Never a whit
> Regards she wealth, though it belie renown's name;
> All to its end she bringeth.

Posterity must pay for the misdoings of its ancestors. The punishment takes the form of blindness (*ate*) and frowardness (*hybris*), which produce a new sin, until the whole line is destroyed; retributive justice watches over the family like a hereditary curse, an idea which Aeschylus developed out of old elements and to which he gave unsurpassed dramatic expression, thus giving his plays such arresting power that modern dramatists come back to them again and again. It is significant that this idea is much weakened in Sophokles, who handled the same material; the old belief would not fit his later and more humane age, for its foundation, the belief that posterity must atone for the ill doings of the older generations, had by that time gone.

Such a view, which seems to us contrary to the natural and right idea that the author of an offence, and only he, ought to pay the penalty for it, could prevail only so long as the individual was regarded merely as a link in the chain of his lineage, and as the kin was regarded as a unity whose members' solidarity made them responsible for each other's actions. The opposite conception, which we think self-evident, had already such convincing power in itself that it came forward as the first sign of the awakening of individualism. The natural demand that the wrongdoer himself, not his children nor his clan, should be punished is already expressed by Solon in a passage which is little more than a parenthesis.

> Or soon or late the punishment alights,
> Or, if some 'scape the destined penalty,
> Yet still it comes; the heavy reckoning smites
> Their race, their *innocent posterity*.

The protest against the old idea lies in the one word 'innocent'. It is not just that the guiltless should be punished for an offence which another has committed. From this point of view, the individual is separated from the chain of the kin. Theognis expresses the same thought with more completeness and emphasis. He prays to Zeus that he who loves

frowardness and commits evil deeds without regarding the
gods may himself undergo the punishment for his actions
and that the misdoings of the father may not be laid upon
his children; that the children of an unrighteous father who
fear the wrath of Zeus, think just thoughts, and from the
beginning practise justice among their fellow citizens, may
not pay the price of their father's transgression. 'May this
be the gods' pleasure! for now the wrongdoer escapes, and
another afterwards suffers ill.'

As this conception gained more and more ground, a difficult, almost insoluble problem arose for the Greeks' firm
belief in the accomplishment of retributive justice. No one
could help seeing that many who committed unjust deeds
and seized goods and estates by injustice died in the peaceful
possession of their property, without being touched by the
penalty they deserved. If their innocent children and family
were freed from the punishment for their misdoings, the
demand for retribution remained unsatisfied, an intolerable,
almost unthinkable idea for Greeks of that age. There was
but one solution; the punishment which does not find the
sinner in this life overtakes him in the other. Beyond a
doubt, the demand for retributive justice to be accomplished
contributed to forming the conceptions already mentioned
concerning punishment in the underworld, which came into
being at that time.

No less a thinker than Plato worked out this thought most
powerfully in conjunction with the doctrine of transmigration. Time and again he turns to mythically coloured
descriptions of the other life, often as the crown and comple-
tion of a work. In him we meet for the first time the three
judges who pass sentence in the underworld upon the actions
of human beings in this life; earlier the myth had appeared
in a different shape. He divides wrongdoers into two classes,
those who can be bettered, and are purified and cleansed
from their misdeeds by means of punishment, and the in-
corrigible, who are hurled into Tartaros and to all eternity

must endure the heaviest and most frightful penalties as a warning to others. The punishment is not an end in itself; it is not revenge, but serves to purify, or at least as a warning, and its basis is the demand for justice; man shall take the just reward of his deeds. Plato was much read, and made his contribution to the belief in the subterranean Hell.

The demand for retributive justice had another side as well as the punishment of the unrighteous; its complement, although it was less talked of, was the reward of the righteous. The pious and just were to spend the other life in joy and mirth; Elysion, in Pindar for example, is described as a veritable Land of Cockaigne. Aristophanes gives vigorous expression to this belief in the song which he puts into the mouth of his chorus of those initiated at Eleusis.

> Now let us to the flowery leas
> Where roses ever grow,
> Plying the dance we know,
> Merriest sport to please
> Those whom a happy fate
> Here bids congregate.

> For us alone a cheerful light
> Shines from the glorious sun,
> Initiates every one,
> Pious in life, upright
> To guests from far and near,
> And to our townsfolk dear.

The older, unsophisticated notion, uninfluenced by the nascent individualism, was that righteousness found its reward in this life. Hesiod declares that Zeus sends famine, plague, and defeat to an unjust people, while those who practise justice enjoy the blessings of peace. In the same way, a righteous house is rewarded with good fortune and prosperity. A righteous man leaves behind flourishing children and grandchildren, whereas the house of the unrighteous is extinguished. We have found this opinion expressed in Aeschylus. For the Greeks it was a disaster, not to die, for that was the inevitable end of life, but to die without leaving behind any descendants who could bring the due offerings to the tombs of their ancestors.

The experience of life showed that such a belief was wrong. Violence and partiality by no means always brought down punishment on the head of the guilty. Since the gods allotted men their fates and Zeus especially was the champion of justice, criticism of life's unfairness was directed against the gods, and against Zeus above all. This criticism of divine justice, whose first hesitant beginnings are to be found in Solon and Theognis, raised its voice loudly in later times, but the archaic period, which had not yet gone so far as to waver in its faith in the gods, took different lines, which we will now attempt to set forth.

4. THE LAW OF APOLLO

We do not know how Apollo's oracle at Delphoi won its pre-eminent position in matters religious and secular during the archaic period in Greece, but we can see that it understood the movements of the time and knew how to adapt itself to them. Apollo encouraged legalism, but ecstatic religion was no stranger to him. The Pythia, his priestess, prophesied in an ecstasy, whereas other oracles gave their answers by different methods. Apollo found room for Dionysos; on one pediment of his temple stood Dionysos with his maenads, on the other Apollo with his sister and mother; Dionysos was worshipped at Delphoi during the three winter months, Apollo during the remaining parts of the year. Apollo did not attempt the hopeless enterprise of suppressing ecstasy; he took it into his service, regularized it, and thus deprived it of its dangerous offshoots. In Apollo's society there appeared extraordinary figures like Abaris and Hermotimos; the affinity between them lay in the fact that they were priests who performed rites of purification. It has been noted that the name Pythagoras means 'mouthpiece of Pytho' (i.e. Delphoi); the Pythagoreans pushed legalism and the demand for purity to their utmost extreme.

In one important connexion, that of purification from blood-guilt, we are allowed to see further into Apollo's activity. Homer's heroes troubled themselves but little about homicide. He tells us of exile and wergeld, but not of guilt nor defilement; but in the mother country a stricter feeling, with its roots in the immemorial past, was prevalent; it is reflected in strange old-fashioned customs, and myths have much to say of the cleansings and purifications which the killing of a man made necessary. Purifications are to be found in the religions of many peoples, including that of Greece, and the decisive point for the religious life is the importance which is attached to them, or the seriousness with which the requirement of purification is taken. If they are not left to the individual's good pleasure but put forward as a binding duty, they are of the greatest consequence for people's religious conduct, for they exercise a deep influence on their whole life. They are still more apt than cult to confine life within fixed religious forms, for they must be attended to whenever there is occasion for them, and they are founded upon a feeling of guilt and impurity which the necessity for purification intensifies and strengthens. The purification may be a mere ceremony, but in the feeling there lies the germ of an ethical conception.

Apollo was above all the god of purifications, but he emphasized with especial vigour the need of purification for those who had burdened themselves with the heaviest pollution, that caused by shedding human blood. Until he was purified, the homicide was debarred from all association with gods and men; he might not be seen among his fellows, nor enter a public place; every house was shut against him; no one ventured to come near him, for his mere touch, even the sight of him, was polluting. It was a stern but wholesome lesson which Apollo inculcated; it was no longer possible to take the destruction of a human life so lightly as

Homer's heroes did. By demanding purification strictly and
without exception, Apollo gave emphasis and weight to the
respect for human life. He himself had shown the way by a
good example, for when he killed the dragon Python, which
guarded Delphoi, he submitted to an elaborate process of
purification.

A homicide was especially serious if it took place within
a place consecrated to the gods. Once the inhabitants of
Sybaris quarrelled with a harp-player and killed him, although
he had taken refuge at an altar of Hera. A portent ensued;
the temple streamed with blood. When the Sybarites sought
counsel of Delphoi, the Pythia chased them away with the
angry utterance,

> Forth from my tripods! Still your murderous hands
> Drip gore and bar you from my marble portal.
> No oracle I give you.

In the negotiations which preceded the Peloponnesian
War, charges of blood-guilt took a prominent place. The
Spartans made reference to the guilt incurred by the Athenians a couple of centuries earlier, in the suppression of
Kylon's attempt to make himself tyrant; the accusation was
levelled at Perikles, a descendant of the men who had taken
the leading part on that occasion. The Athenians in their
turn called upon the Spartans to atone for the guilt they had
incurred by killing refugees who had sought shelter in the
temple of Poseidon at Tainaron and by letting Pausanias,
the victor of Plataiai, starve to death in the temple of Athena
Chalkioikos and burying his body close by. The oracle had
already enjoined a penance upon them for that offence.

These events prove how much alive the feeling of blood-
guilt was at a quite late date; we now return to the archaic
period, when Apollo was busy insisting upon the pollution
of blood-guilt and the necessity for purification. He co-
operated with the States in their effort to do away with
blood-revenge, which gave rise to endless feuds, and take

the infliction of punishment into their own hands. The States themselves, for their own sakes, must see to it that homicide was atoned for, because if that were not done, the wrath of the gods fell upon the whole people. When the Athenians stoned a begging priest who was propagandizing for the Asian Mother of the Gods, and threw his body into the pit where the corpses of criminals were cast, a pestilence broke out; the oracle told them to make purification for his death and build a temple to the Mother of the Gods. This event took place towards the end of the sixth century, not, as is commonly said, at the beginning of the Peloponnesian War. The formalities for a trial for homicide show a close association with religious rites, and also were so complicated that special experts (*exegetaí*) had to be called in to conduct them properly. Plato, in his *Laws*, still describes these formalities and prescribes exact attention to them.

Purifications were needed on many occasions in life, but we may content ourselves with one further instance. Even fire might become unclean. When the Persians, during their invasion of Greece, ruined and violated the sanctuaries of the gods, but in the end were defeated at the Battle of Plataiai and driven out, clean fire was brought from Delphoi to light the altars for the sacrifice made after the victory. A similar rite is the brilliant procession in which the Athenians, at a much later time, used to fetch pure fire from Delphoi. In Apollo's worship we often find officials with the title of 'firebearer'.

All that has hitherto been dealt with in connexion with the demand for ritual purity is legalism; but Apollo by no means took up the position that a man might do as he chose and clear himself of guilt by performing the prescribed purifications. He rose to a demand for inward purity as well. There is an incident in Herodotos which is often cited. A Spartan called Glaukos, son of Epikydes, had undertaken the custody of a sum of money belonging to a Milesian. The latter died and after a long while his heirs appeared and asked

for the money back. But Glaukos would not remember that
he had taken charge of any money. He asked the oracle if
he could clear himself by taking an oath and the Pythia
answered:

> Thy present profit, Epikydes' son,
> Bids swear and win thy cause and seize the gold.
> So swear; for e'en the oathfast man must die.
> Howbeit, the Oath-god hath a nameless son,
> Handless and footless, yet he follows fast
> Till in his clutch both house and kin expire.
> Better his offspring fare who keeps his oath.

Glaukos was contrite and begged for pardon, but the Pythia
answered that to tempt the deity and to commit an evil deed
amounted to the same thing. And, Herodotos adds, Glaukos'
house is extinct in Sparta, and there is no family and no man
who claims descent from him.

Apollo associated himself with and promoted the powerful
movements which, in that age of unrest and ferment, tried
to bring about peace, order, and law. For the age in which
his oracle gained its leading position was one of great material
and political development, of social disorder and unrest, of
class-conflict, a time which inevitably needed reforms in law
and constitution. That was the age which saw the great
legislators; the first demand, that the laws, hitherto handed
down by word of mouth, should be reduced to writing,
necessarily brought with it another, for the reform of those
laws. In the most progressive States the tyrants who came
into power based it upon the unprivileged and discontented
classes; their power did not last long, but it emphasized the
need of reforms. The law rested on a religious foundation
not only in its ordinances concerning murder and homicide.
The centuries in which Greek jurisprudence was shaped were
agitated by important religious movements. In proportion
as these brought about new ethical demands, they had also
a controlling influence in the development of laws, but it was
particularly the case that oracles and myths were generally

recognized as the standard of right for human activities. Thus to a great extent religion and law were two different forms of expression of the same power which was active in the life of the people.

If this is clearly understood, it is easier to comprehend the much talked-of influence of Apollo upon the legislation of that day. He was the divine authority to which recourse was had for regulating or, when necessary, reforming a cult. He gave recognition to new gods and heroes (we may say he canonized the latter), and to alterations in established worships. He regulated the cults of settlers who were going out to found a city in foreign parts. He sanctioned regulations for festivals, with which the introduction of an ordered calendar, which he favoured, was closely connected, for the hundreds of Greek names of months (they varied from one State to the next) are almost without exception derived from the names of festivals celebrated in them. He extended his activity from sacral to civil law. It is a mistake to understand this, as is sometimes done, as meaning that Apollo prescribed laws and statutes, but the States had recourse to him and asked for his sanction for the laws which their legislators had recorded or given, and Apollo thus gave the civil law his support by right of his divine authority. Now and then it happened that he appointed a legislator. In the middle of the sixth century serious disturbances took place in Kyrene and the situation grew so desperate that the inhabitants turned to the oracle and besought its advice. Apollo bade them get a legislator from Mantineia, and that city sent them its most prominent man, Demonax. Apollo secured his position as interpreter of the age's need and demand for law and justice, for firm rules which should uphold peace in society. He could do this because his first business was to secure peace with the gods by proclaiming, interpreting, and enforcing their commandments.

In a time of social distress and turmoil, which fomented religious distress and turbulence, men felt their consciences

Human law which was written down & reformed rested upon divine authority, and there was the more need of that authority to make peace with the gods

THE LAW OF APOLLO   47

pricked by transgressions, deliberate or otherwise, of the divine commands, and their feelings caught by new religious longings and strivings. They were looking for a safe anchorage, a sure road. The wrath of the gods revealed itself in the misfortunes of the age, and human skill was not enough to avert or expiate them. Human law which was written down and reformed rested upon divine authority, and there was the more need of that authority to make peace with the gods.

5. KNOW THYSELF

Man must not tempt the gods; he must know his place and subordinate himself to their will. This lesson was inculcated in sundry myths shaped under Delphic influence and meant to insist upon the certainty that the utterances of the oracle find fulfilment, whatever efforts man may make to evade it. The oracle had warned Laios, king of Thebes, against begetting a son, and foretold that if he did so, he would die by his son's hand. Laios did not obey, but when he had a son, he caused him to be exposed, with a hole bored through his feet (whence he came to be called Oidipus, 'Swell-foot') in a desert place, so that he might perish. The child was rescued and grew up in Corinth to a strong young man. When the youth went to Delphoi to ask about his birth, the oracle warned him not to return home. Instead of returning to Corinth, he took the road to Thebes and met, without knowing it, his father in a narrow place. A quarrel arose from a trifling cause, and ended with Oidipus, in a rage, killing his father. The lesson of the myth is to the effect, not only that we should not doubt the word of a god, but still more that we should obey the gods, be submissive to them, and bow unquestioningly before their will.

Inscribed on Apollo's temple at Delphoi was the famous saying *gnothi seautón*, 'know thyself'. No saying has been so often repeated. For us, it signifies the need for self-knowledge; for its own time it meant, 'know that you are human and nothing more'. That saying is the kernel of the doctrine concerning man's relation to the gods on which Apollo insisted. Mankind is to be conscious of its own impotence and the power of the gods, and submit to them. Together with this saying Plato mentions *medèn agan*, 'nothing too much', and in another passage he savs that the visitor to Apollo's temple was met by the advice *sophrónei*. The Greek conception which is contained in this word is hard to render; one might perhaps say, 'Be wise', in the sense of showing wise moderation, knowing one's place, and not displaying haughtiness towards gods or men. The content of the saying is like that of 'nothing too much'. Pindar expresses the same thought more strongly with his warning; if fortune is kind to you, 'seek not to become Zeus'. Never forget the impassable gulf between gods and men. The same dislike of all excess lies at the bottom of Apollo's well-known enmity to the tyrants who were then in power in numerous States; they were men who did as they liked, made a display of their power and wealth, and set up to be supermen; the very opposite of Apollo's ideal. He could but fight them.

Later authors give us various accounts which throw light on the sort of piety which Apollo would have men show in their relations with the gods. Once, when a man from Thessaly brought a hecatomb of victims with gilded horns, the Pythia declared that a man from Hermione, who had offered, with three fingers, a little meal from his bag, had brought an offering more acceptable to the gods. When the man from Hermione heard of this and emptied the whole bag on the altar, the Pythia rebuked him and said that he was twice as hateful to the gods as he had formerly been well-pleasing. The same doctrine is inculcated by the anecdote of the Sicilian tyrants, who after a victory over the Carthaginians brought hecatombs to the god and asked, not without a thought for themselves, in which offering the deity took most pleasure. He answered, in a few pinches of meal which a poor husbandman had offered in passing. A third account is still more instructive. A man of Magnesia in Asia Minor, who every year prepared handsome sacrifices for the gods, brought a hecatomb to Delphoi; believing that he showed his reverence for the gods better than anyone else, he asked who did the gods the best and readiest honour. The Pythia replied, 'Klearchos of Methydrion'. Astonished, the Magnesian went to the little place where Klearchos lived, and found a man who, at the proper times, every day of new moon, cleaned and garlanded the statues of Hermes and Hekate—that is domestic worship—offered incense and cakes in the sanctuaries, and took part in the yearly festivals of the gods without missing one.

We may call such piety ritualism, to which indeed Apollo was no stranger, but that is not the whole truth. Nor is it right to make a comparison between these anecdotes and the story in the Gospels about the widow's mite which was best pleasing to God. The intention is not to condemn wealth in itself, any more than poverty is in itself a merit; the god took a dislike to the poor man of Hermione when he emptied his whole bag on the altar. The doctrine inculcated is that man is not to be boastful of his piety nor make a show of it; he is to be humble before the gods. The thought of his duties towards the gods must leaven his life so completely and utterly that he fulfils them almost without thinking, like Klearchos. The piety which Apollo wanted, like that of Hesiod, fills the whole of life, and both demand exact and regular attention to ritual rules and commands. The two are closely related, children of the same period.

These anecdotes are handed down by Theophrastos, the pupil of Aristotle, but we cannot doubt that they go back to the archaic period. There is a related story concerning Myson, who is mentioned as early as Hipponax, a poet who lived in the middle of the sixth century B.C. Hipponax calls Myson *sophronestatos*, the most prudent or moderate of all. A later anecdote makes Anacharsis ask the oracle if anyone were wiser than himself; Apollo referred him to Myson. In the poor village where Myson lived, Anacharsis found him, a peasant who was mending a plough on a summer's day. When Anacharsis told him that that was no time to be ploughing, Myson replied, 'No, but it is the time to mend the plough.' That is the whole story. It contains not a hint of religious duties, but the spirit of it is the same as in the other anecdotes; a man must not be proud, but realize his own littleness and do everything at the right time. Myson was accounted one of the Seven Sages.

In these anecdotes we possess remains of a folk-literature of archaic date in which this spirit is reflected. Other remains are to be found in stories about the famous Seven Sages, which have been called folk-novellas, and are a veritable catchment for the proverbial wisdom of the time. Hipparchos, son of Peisistratos, tyrant of Athens, had herms set up along the roads of Attica by way of milestones, with maxims engraved on them:

> Hipparchos' rede; keep justice in thy mind.
> Hipparchos' rede; deceive not thou thy friend.

Combined with sayings which have a religious or moral tendency are others of pure worldly wisdom. The fourth of the Delphic sayings which Plato mentions may be rendered 'who goes a-borrowing, goes a-sorrowing'.

These maxims, whether religious, moral, or practical, form an inseparable unity. Such a saying as *medèn agan*, 'nothing too much', 'avoid excess', signifies in a religious sense the doctrine which Apollo inculcated in the examples we have given, the doctrine of man's humility before the gods. But in its political tendency it was the wisdom of the statesman seeking to put down the ruinous strife between classes. The saying is also an expression of the ripe philosophy of life produced by the last centuries of the archaic period. Alongside the fermenting unrest and the many new and contentious enterprises in all departments of life there ran the strong movement which sought for order, asked that man should realize his limitations and know his place in relation

both to the gods and to his fellows, that he should attend to
and take seriously the commands which are necessary for the
preservation of peace with the gods and peace within human
society, without which there cannot be a peaceable and
regulated communal life.

This movement is legalistic; this was a necessary means for
quieting the unrest of the times, so that the revolutionary
movements should not degenerate in the final result into
the collapse of society and religion, but that there should
crystallize out of them a practicable order of society and
religious atmosphere. This movement found expression in
Hesiod's rules for life, in the practical wisdom of the Seven
Sages, which prescribed rules for human dealings and for
the relations of men to the gods and to each other; in the
legislation which began by writing down the orally trans-
mitted law and ended with radical reforms of the State and
society; in the directions of the oracle for the regulation of
the religious life. The object of practical wisdom and of
legislation was to set up peace among men; that of Apollo,
to preserve peace with the gods.

The legalistic movement was not Apollo's doing; it sprang
from the sane instinct of the people and achieved importance
as the necessary counterpoise to the unrest of the age.
Apollo took it over, founded his power upon it, and advanced
it powerfully through his divine authority, starting from
ordinances for cult. His limitation was that he was one of
the Olympian gods. Their standpoint was his, and he therefore could not fashion a really new religious growth. His
advice was regularly 'follow the law of the State', 'follow
the customs of your fathers'. Some things were beneath his
dignity, such as Hesiod's and the Pythagoreans' tabus,
which if systematically extended and based on divine
authority might have held not merely a sect but all his
people in the bond of a ceremonial law. The Greek gods
did their people the service of not troubling about the many
petty details of life, so long as the demands of cult were

satisfied. The Greeks escaped the shackles of ceremonial law.

6. *HYBRIS* AND *NEMESIS*

The movement which took the strongest possession of men's minds in the archaic age of Greece was the struggle for justice—justice in the social, moral, and religious sense. From that sprang legalism. Apollo turned this movement to account, but never understood its profundity nor its extent, and could not understand it, because he was an Olympian. He left on one side the question which must necessarily obtrude itself, and did so, the question of the justice of the gods' dealings and of the fate which they caused to overtake mankind. Instead, he taught the lesson of man's humility before the gods, his duty of submitting to the gods' decision without asking how it was justified. Apollo did not appropriate the kernel of the Greek conception of justice, which was righteous retribution. The struggle for justice was fought out on the social plane, and the consequences affected religious feeling as well.

Hybris and *nemesis* are two well-known Greek words, a pair of concepts which we find as far back as Homer. *Hybris* is haughtiness in word and deed, presumption, presumptuous conduct; *nemesis* is the ill will or indignation which such conduct arouses. *Hybris* is connected with the Homeric phrase *hypèr moron*, usually translated 'beyond fate', an expression which involves a self-contradiction; the real meaning is 'beyond the allotted portion'. For the Homeric words *moira* and *aisa*, usually translated 'fate', signify 'allotment', 'portion', for example a share of booty or a 'helping' at a meal, and hence the regular, proper share which falls to a man's lot; he can lay hold of more than this, take 'above his portion', and this, in a later age, is *hybris*. From the idea of orderliness which is contained in the above-mentioned words develops the idea of destiny, which takes a fatalistic colouring from the consciousness that man's assured 'portion' is death, which not even the gods can avert. The conceptions of destiny and of the omnipotence of the gods were on different planes, but the beginnings of the insoluble problem of the conflict between them appear now and again even in Homer. However, the Homeric fatalism was of no importance for the age immediately following him.

The conception of *hybris* was developed and more clearly defined by the introduction of a new idea, *koros*. This word means satiety, but without the connotation of disgust which the English word is apt to have; it connotes abundant access to the good things of life, property, power, and enjoyment, such as for instance the dynasts of that age had. Solon says that satiety brings forth *hybris*, and Theognis that it has destroyed more men than hunger, men who wanted to have more than their proper portion. Haughtiness provokes indignation and should be punished, and therefore the ideas concerning *hybris* and *nemesis* were united with the conception of just retribution which governed the archaic period.

For retributive justice, as the Greeks understood it, held good not only in law and jurisdiction but also in social life, in human life in general, and occasionally in Nature as well, and took on the meaning of equalizing justice, of a levelling-out. It was for such justice that the political battles were fought; the catchword *isonomía* meant not only equality before the law, but also an equal share in the good things the State apportions to its citizens, whether material or immaterial. This idea was deeply rooted; it was the motor force in the constitutional contest and the foundation of democracy, which aimed at equality. No one could ignore it, however energetically he fought against it. And so it was that the concept of *hybris* and *nemesis* changed into an expression for equalizing justice, in so far as that manifested itself in the lot of man with its variations between good and evil fortune; and also, that this whole complex of ideas had to be brought face to face with the belief in the gods' intervention in and guidance of human destiny.

The answer to the question in what manner the gods intervene in human life was gathered from the varying fortunes of our existence; good luck does not last. Herodotos speaks of a 'wheel' in human fortunes, which revolves continually and will not let the same man always have fortune on his side. The reason for this change between good luck and bad was found in man's *hybris* and the gods' *nemesis*. This doctrine became influential in the days before the Persian War, when the ancient nobility was losing its power and wealth and parvenus won and lost property and position, tyrants usurped power and then were overthrown and killed. The fifth-century democracy made the upper classes undergo a like insecurity. The sense of the incalculability of fate hung threateningly over the heads of mankind.

What was the reason of fate's incalculability? The archaic period lived in the belief that haughtiness was punished with a corresponding measure of suffering, and *hybris* was haughtiness, or over-confidence. No one, however, could avoid seeing that a man might have good fortune without harbouring over-confidence or showing overweening pride. So under *hybris* was included the mere fact of good fortune itself, or perhaps we should rather say the feeling of having good fortune on one's side; a transition from a moral idea to a philosophy of life which might be called objective.

It was the gods who sent destinies; they were the origin of the changes of fortune. The question of the justice of their governance presented itself clamorously. Theognis expresses his astonishment that Zeus, who rules omnipotent over all and surely knows the thoughts of men, lets the wicked and the good meet the same fate, and that an unjust fate befalls the righteous, while the unrighteous escape the divine wrath. Components of various dates have been included in the collection of verses which pass under Theognis' name, so that we cannot declare with certainty that this passage is of his age, but it is not unlikely that criticism of the divine government of the universe was aroused even at that early time.

Later authors took up the pious attitude that the gods are so much exalted above men that the latter must not question the justice of their dealings. Sophokles represents Athena as smiting Aias with madness and puts the following words into her mouth:

> Gaze on this sight, and let no boastful word
> Fall ever from thy lips against the gods,
> Neither wax proud, if strength of hand be thine
> More than another's, or abundant wealth.
> A day lays low, a day may raise again
> All that is human, and the gods still love
> The prudent heart and hate the sinful man.

From these postulates Pindar developed a philosophy of life in an ode written for Hieron, tyrant of Syracuse, at a time when he was afflicted by an illness.

For one blessing, the Immortals give to man a double portion of sorrow. Fools cannot bear it off with a brave show, but only the noble heart, by turning the fair side outermost. . . . Well may that mortal man who keeps in mind the world's true course, have comfort of the fair lot that falls to him by heaven's grace. But the winged winds of the height blow changefully with changing time. Man's fortune voyages not far unshipwrecked, when its burden is too deeply laden. As are the days of great and small things, so will I be great or small. . . . From the powers above us must we seek what is our due, since our mortal thoughts know but that which lies before our feet, such is our portion. Seek not, my heart, for immortal life, but rather accept what thou mayest have.

It is the old lesson, 'know thyself'—know that you are no more than human, that an impassable barrier stands between gods and men. This view reaches its highest development in Sophokles. His Oidipus, who falls from the loftiest heights of power and good fortune to unspeakable misery, is the greatest and most arresting example of human impotence and the gods' unescapable dooms. The poet extends this idea even to the State, which is no more obliged than the gods to account for its doings to the individual. Antigone puts her religious duties above the command of her State, but she must also endure what the State inflicts upon her. So Sokrates thought, and showed it in his behaviour at the time of his death.

Except for Sokrates, there is no question of an ethical basis for good or ill fortune. That is sent by the gods, and the gods are not obliged to give mankind a reasoned account. But when the feeling for justice, formal justice at least, made itself effective, the idea of *nemesis* took a new form, that a portion of good luck is counterbalanced by an equal portion of ill luck, a doctrine which was read into the course of history. Kroisos, Polykrates, Xerxes, all of them powerful and glorious princes, but all smitten with the heaviest strokes of misfortune, served as examples of this favourite maxim. In Herodotos we find the idea current of an equalization which takes place through the balancing of great good fortune with great ill fortune. In his famous introduction in which he states the subject of his historical work, the conflict between the Orient and Greece, the guiding thought is that one injustice is repaid by another. His story about Polykrates is especially valuable because it is a piece of folk-literature, to be found also in modern folk-tales. Amasis, king of Egypt, wrote a letter to Polykrates, tyrant of Samos, who was attended by persistent good fortune, in which he advised him to throw away something which he especially valued, in order to balance the account. Polykrates took his advice, and threw a valuable ring into the sea. When Amasis afterwards heard that the ring had been found in the belly of a fish which a fisherman had brought to Polykrates, he renounced his friendship with him, for he thought it dangerous to be friendly with a man who was so pursued by good fortune. And Polykrates came to a bad end, being crucified by a Persian satrap.

The notion of the balancing of the variations of fortune had a popular foundation in the conception of *baskania*, that praise causes ill luck; this is connected with the belief in the destructive power of the evil eye, which is still held by southern nations. So with us it is customary, in speaking of something which has gone remarkably well, to add 'touch wood'. Such praise with its attendant ill fortune was avoided by an attitude of self-depreciation, for instance by spitting in one's bosom. Herodotos expresses a similar belief when he says that Kroisos was assailed by the *nemesis* of the gods because he thought himself the most fortunate of all men. He elsewhere expresses the Greek conception when he makes Artabanos the Persian expound to Xerxes how the gods smite the largest creatures with their thunderbolts and will not let them think highly of themselves, but are not vexed with the small ones; that lightning always strikes the loftiest palaces and the highest trees, 'for it is God's way to cut short everything that rises high'. Herakleitos the philosopher said that it is more needful to quench *hybris* than to put out a house on fire.

The feeling that one has good fortune on his side is frowardness, *hybris*, for it transcends the boundary fixed for man; it sins against the maxim *medèn agan*, 'nothing too much'. Aristotle analyses this conception in a truly Greek spirit.

Those who think themselves extraordinarily fortunate [he says] do not feel pity, but are overbearing; for if they think that all good things are theirs, it is obvious that they count on it being impossible for them to meet with any ill, since this also is one of the good things.

He is trying to give a psychological explanation of the view that too great good fortune is vainglory.

On the other hand, the idea that the gods like to strike down whatever rises higher than the rest gave rise to the opinion that they did so out of envy, *phthonos*, which perhaps had better be translated 'ill will', since 'envy' suggests moral inferiority. Pindar wishes that when, with a song, he fits the wreath upon the victor's brow, the envy of the immortals may not shatter him, and in another passage, that those who have had for their portion no small amount of good fortune may not be overtaken by envious changes sent by the gods.

In the famous conversation which Herodotos puts into the mouths of Solon and Kroisos at their meeting, it is stated that when Kroisos praised his own good fortune, Solon replied that deity is jealous and likes to cause violent upheavals. Even though *phthonos* is used indifferently with *nemesis*, still the former word has an unpleasant sound. The conception of *hybris* and *nemesis* is alive for Herodotos, but his characters, though not himself, speak oftener of the envy of the gods; here *phthonos* can indeed be translated 'envy', since they voice the popular idea which ascribed the misfortunes of life to a wholly human envy on the part of the gods rather than that philosophy of life which extracted from experience the conclusion that good and ill fortune balance each other. Sometimes he adopts the unmerciful opinion that the gods beguile men into *hybris* in order to punish them in the interests of the world-order.

Such a view as we have described must lead to quietism, for, since the greatest are the most exposed to the blows of fate, it is best to be one of the small. Myson, whom Apollo considered the wisest of all, was a simple peasant. This leads in turn to pessimism. For, since life yields twice as much evil as good, the conclusion must follow (and the Greeks often gave it utterance but never applied it) that it is best never to be born and next-best to die young. This wisdom was the price for which Midas set Seilenos free when he had been so fortunate as to catch him; we find it in Theognis and the tragedians and in Herodotos, in the dialogue between Solon and Kroisos which is so characteristic for that view of life, and in the former's story of Kleobis and Biton. When the mother of these two young men prayed to the gods to reward their filial piety with the best that could befall a human being, they fell sweetly asleep in the temple and never awoke. Their tale is an old one, for statues of the pair have been found at Delphoi, dating from the first half of the sixth century.

We may with propriety ask if the ideas of *hybris* and

nemesis really deserve to be called religious. It was a philosophy of life, put together from experience of the changes of fortune and the incertitude of our existence, of the wheel in human destiny, from the firm belief in retributive justice, and from a good deal of fatalism. Towards that naïve fatalism which holds that what will be, will be, which Homer already adopts, Herodotos has a consistent leaning; obviously it was familiar in his time. It is not surprising that fatalism made a contribution to the idea of *hybris* and *nemesis*, for *nemesis* is at the same time a fate which man cannot avoid, and fatalism is merely another name for what is put forward as the content of that conception, an objective handling of the chances and changes of life. Thus we also can understand better why this idea did not cripple the Greeks' activity; such naïve fatalism does not; on the contrary, it can strengthen it.

The gods were given as much room as possible; they were the almighty ones who, without considering guilt or desert, dealt out men's fates to them. This has been called an objective view of life, but from the religious standpoint it was but a poor remnant. It was a jejune wisdom, good enough for wearily resigned people, and the only reason why it held its ground was that the Greeks did not practise what they preached. The Greeks of that day were neither wearied nor resigned, and the view they took of life did not prevent them from enjoying it to the full. The paean in praise of action which Herodotos represents Xerxes as uttering in answer to Artabanos' doubts is also derived from Greek views.

7. DEITY

In Homer we find a remarkable contrast between the poet's description of what happens and the narratives of the characters in the story. While the poet always knows which god intervened, and gives his name, those who tell of their experiences never do so, but speak vaguely of a god, a daimon, or the gods in general as responsible for what has happened. Even if they name Zeus, his name does not signify the god who sits on Olympos and sends the lightning; the name of the chief god has become so generalized in its connotation as to signify no more than 'a god' or 'the gods'. Homer uses the word *daimon* of his anthropomorphic deities, who have a marked individuality, but still oftener it means an indefinite divine power which has no clear individual character, except what it gets from the momentary manifestation of the visitations it sends. It is the power which lies behind the particular events. Therefore a general, undefined expression such as 'a god' or 'the gods' may be used instead of *daimon*, and the all-inclusive nature of the chief god may be so enhanced that the name of Zeus becomes synonymous with such a general expression.

The reason for this remarkable peculiarity is not hard to understand. The poet had in his hands what we usually call the 'divine apparatus' of Homer, the intervention of the gods in matters great and small, but an ordinary person had not. The ordinary man had no particular connexion with any god, he could not know which god in any particular instance took a hand in the confusing multiplicity of happenings. Very often we are told that a daimon brings a man somewhere against his will or intention, or contrary to expectation. Quite often a daimon is mentioned as the cause of a sudden impulse. Since the mainsprings of action lie hidden in the depths of the soul, it is not so constituted that a man can refer to a definite, individual god as giving rise to it. Often he feels as though some obscure power led him, went against his intentions, and brought him to a result which he neither expected nor wanted. That power cannot be one of the individual gods, but a dark, indefinite, unknown supernatural power, a daimon.

This idea is Homeric; in later times it faded, but not without leaving a trace behind. The application of the word *daimon* to the great gods was restricted, and it was principally employed in reference to lesser gods and indefinite supernatural powers. In the Attic orators we note a manifest

tendency to ascribe ill fortune to a daimon; they hesitated
to make the gods responsible for it. This is the beginning of
the deterioration of the word which finally led to its getting
the meaning which 'demon' has in our language.

In the period after Homer, we seldom hear of the conception of the undefined supernatural power which mani-
fests itself in a particular visitation and is its cause, but it
did not disappear altogether, and a similar conception made
its appearance with the emergence of the ideas which have
just been described. The levelling out of the total of the
different chances which man meets with, so that ill luck
counterbalances good luck, could not be ascribed to any
particular god but formed part of the divine government of
the universe. Hence they spoke of 'the god', 'the gods', 'the
divine', 'deity', as its origin; as in Homer, Zeus might replace
this general expression, for the name of the chief god became
so generalized as to mean no more than that. The word
daimon changed its meaning; except in poetry, it was hardly
used any more as synonymous with 'a god', and so on, but
on the other hand periphrases such as 'the daimonic' cor-
responded to 'the divine'. *Daimon* also meant, occasionally,
much the same as 'fate'. There soon appeared another word
as a rival to the former, this being *tyche*. *Tyche* is connected
with a verb which signifies 'hit (a mark), happen, reach, get
to (something)'; its primary meaning is 'that which happens'. The word is usually rendered 'fortune' or 'luck', but
can also mean 'ill luck'. We must remember the purely
objective meaning of the word, which may be expressed by
the phrase 'the way things go'. We shall meet with it again;
but its personification, which did not become important
until later, is of no consequence here. Furthermore, there
was the old word for fate, *moira*.

We can trace in the writers of the fifth century how this
general conception of the divine powers which guide us
expanded more and more, and at the same time narrowed.
Aeschylus, who was deeply religious, brings fate (*moira*) into

connexion with Zeus or the gods, or identifies it with Zeus' decision; that in his tragedy of *Prometheus* fate is an unavoidable destiny which even Zeus cannot set aside is a result of the dramatic situation. Aeschylus' conviction was that the gods, and above all Zeus, govern the world and send our fortunes, whether bad or good, and when he speaks in more detail on the subject he always emphasizes guilt and justice; justice comes from Zeus, whose daughter Dike is a personification of the god's righteousness. He often glorifies the omnipotence and the righteousness of Zeus together. This elevation of Zeus to an omnipotent and ethical power is what is called Aeschylus' Zeus-religion, which at the same time maintains Zeus' personality. Since equalizing justice comes from Zeus, the result is that when Aeschylus speaks of it he seldom uses the generic terms 'a god' or 'the gods'.

His younger competitor Sophokles was pious; for him religion was not a problem but a self-evident postulate, forming the background for the subject to which his interest as a dramatist was mainly directed, the doings of mankind, how they act, suffer, and feel as human beings. That stands in the foreground of his picture, however it may be dominated by the divine background, whereas Aeschylus on the contrary uses the fortunes of men to set forth the doings of the gods. It is self-evident that in Sophokles also Zeus keeps his sovran position; he sees everything, directs everything, and Justice stands at his side. That was an ancient inheritance, which was more and more suppressed by the idea of divine powers in general. Sophokles expresses in powerful language the variations of our lot and the instability of fortune, but does not adopt the mechanical equalization which is implied in the double conception of *hybris* and *nemesis*. He seldom uses the latter word, and *hybris* in his writings is always directed against the gods. Only very rarely does he make a god intervene in person, but often speaks of deity, a god, or the gods in general. He expresses the idea of the mutability of fortune by saying that the same daimon does not always

stand at a man's side. An annihilating blow is sent by a god;
the gods send all men their fate. If a god sends misfortune,
even the strong cannot avoid it; a god hurls a man to destruction; a god sends sickness. Still more worn down is an
expression which can be rendered correctly only by a para-
phrase; it means 'the god-sent destiny which is present for
the occasion'. A related expression is 'the present daimon',
in which daimon means simply fate or destiny. To express
the unstable lot of man Sophokles also employs the word
tyche; that *tyche* is sometimes said to have been sent by the
gods is due to the fact that the opposition between the
inevitability of fate and the divine government has not yet
been clearly grasped. Sophokles was pious, but his was not
a profoundly religious nature like that of Aeschylus, and
therefore he could follow the opinions of his time regarding
the gods' government of the universe.

A kindred spirit to Sophokles was the Father of History,
Herodotos. Although he now and then was influenced by
the rationalistic criticism which was beginning to be directed
against gods and society, current conceptions left their mark
on his work. His *leitmotiv* is the changes of fortune and the
instability of prosperity; he coined the expression 'the wheel
in human destiny'. He speaks of Tyche, who can bring man's
life to a good end, can turn good counsel into its opposite,
but can also help bad counsel to a good issue. Blind fate he
speaks of only on isolated occasions; the divine power appears
usually as the author of destiny. In such a context he never
speaks of any particular god, not even of Zeus, but always
employs the generic expression 'a god' or 'the gods', or the
like. In fate he sees the hand of deity, without putting the
question what the relation is between unavoidable destiny
and the power of the gods. Herodotos had not lost belief in
the gods, but they recede into the background, grow shadowy,
and reduce to a general, impersonal divine power, whenever
he speaks of the governance of the world and the destiny
of man.

With Euripides, the criticism and debates of the age of enlightenment made their way upon the stage. He knew the old opinions and expressions and applied them, but it is often hard to tell how much lies behind them, for dramatic technique demands that on occasion words shall be put into the mouths of the characters in the play which are not spoken from the heart of the poet. One might gather an abundant anthology of contradictory utterances from Euripides' plays, and from his numerous fragments, which are still harder to judge, because they are torn from their context. Sometimes he contents himself with merely stating the mutability of life, but often explains, or seems to explain, its origin with the well-known words *moira*, *tyche*, 'gods' or 'deity'. The last two words, which were acquiring an increasingly generalized sense in the older writers, lost still more of their content in him, and sank to a mere form of speech for expressing the fact that good and ill fortune change. Also, for him the problem of the relation between inevitable fate and the omnipotence of the gods comes forward in all its sharpness. The two are incompatible; if there is such a thing as fate, then the gods are superfluous, but if the gods bear rule, fate is nothing.

The philosophy of life which the Greeks constructed on the basis of their experiences of the instability of mortal destiny and the mutations of fortune was from the very beginning connected with their religious belief, because it is the gods who apportion men their destiny; but the universality of the thought called imperatively, so to speak, for a common denominator. A particular god or goddess, or a particular group of gods, could not be made responsible for the general course of destiny. So reference was made to the gods generally, or a god, or deity, a generic expression which lacked personality, life, and vividness. We have traced the paling and thinning of this generic idea, until it interchanges with expressions for destiny or fate and is not much more than a statement of the way things go. There is a very characteristic expression which Thucydides attributes to Perikles: 'what heaven sends (*ta daimonia*) must be borne as of necessity, hostile action met bravely'.

This generalized idea may be called 'deity', but it did not point the way to any monotheistic belief. It is an impersonal abstraction, inaccessible to hopes and prayers, and at the same time stands for unescapable destiny. Human beings cannot be satisfied with such a deity; they look for gods on whom they may rest their hopes and from whom they may seek for grace; they want help and comfort from their gods. This feeble reflection of religious feeling could not stand up against criticism when that began.

Criticism was directed against the old gods, who were personalities with flesh and blood, as we may venture to say in dealing with Greek anthropomorphism. The common people still turned to them, but the educated let their philosophy of life rob religion of its innermost content. Their attitude to religion was ambiguous, even apart from the fact that they held fast to cult. Herodotos, who regularly speaks of *hybris* and *nemesis* and also of deity, has much to tell us of marvellous happenings by which the gods manifested their anger and punished those who had offended against them, and still more of omens, oracles, and their fulfilment.

II

THE DISSOLUTION

I. PATRIOTIC RELIGION

AFTER the victory over the Persians at Salamis and
Plataiai Themistokles declared: 'It is not we who have
done this, but the gods and heroes.' He was right. The
victory was the victory of the Greek gods. Apollo's demand
for law and moderation had contributed to lay the social
unrest and the conflicts within the communities, and the
national exaltation swept away the archaic period's inclination towards mysticism and ecstasy. The gods of the State
had granted the victory, and religion became even more
closely attached to the State than ever. Collective religion
silenced the protest which the demands of individual religion
had raised in the memorable religious movements of the
archaic age.

The gods received their reward. The Greeks forgot
Apollo's ambiguous attitude and set up the national monu-
ment of victory at Delphoi. In Olympia, the great temple
of Zeus, the statue in which was the most famous work of
Pheidias, was erected. The gods' protecting hands were held
over Athens for the next fifty years, the time of the Athenian
Empire. On the Akropolis arose Iktinos' masterpiece, the
Parthenon, decorated with Pheidias' imperishable art, while
his statue of the tutelary goddess of Athens, wrought of gold
and ivory, stood in the cella. Later, the Erechtheion was
built to replace the old temple of the age of Solon and
Peisistratos, which the Persians had burned. Human habita-
tions were cleared away from the Akropolis, the whole of
which was consecrated to the gods. Beneath, in the city,
Hephaistos, the god of artificers, received a large temple
which is still well preserved. The festivals were celebrated
with lavish splendour and brilliance, so many beasts being
sacrificed that the meat was enough to give the whole people

a festal dinner. The theatre in Dionysos' sacred precinct at the foot of the Akropolis, where plays were produced at his feasts, became a school for that day and for posterity. It was perfectly natural that the Athenians should be proud of what they had accomplished and what the grace of the gods had given them, perhaps also because Athens became the centre of the intellectual life of Hellas. What was thought and said there spread over the whole Greek world; thither, as by magnetic attraction, were drawn all who had intellectual interests. For the next two centuries, the history of Greek thought and religion is chiefly the history of Athens.

Patriotism found its expression in the form of religion. Athena was the symbol of the honour of Athens, her power and glory. If patriotic religious feeling has its basis in the State, that means, according to Sam Wide, not an abstract idea of the State but all the good things, material and immaterial, which the State gives, the personal freedom of her citizens and their self-esteem, the political rights which they exercised as members of the sovran democracy, the blessings of peace, and the honourable contest for their ancestral city, the daily bread which the State gave even to the poor and infirm, participation in the many splendid festivals which the State provided, and in the magnificent products of culture, such as science, literature, and art offered in the intellectual centre of the world of that day. All that has been said refers to Athens, but it is possible that a reflection of a similar religion of patriotism, perhaps in a somewhat lesser degree, developed in other States as well. Thucydides makes Perikles express such an idea in the famous oration which he delivered over those who fell during the first year of the Peloponnesian War. In the one reference to religion to be found in that profoundly thoughtful utterance, he says, 'Furthermore, we have provided our minds with very many occasions of rest from labour by means of the contests and sacrifices which it is our custom to celebrate year by year.'

All this is quite true, but the handsome medal has its reverse. The Athenians boasted that they were the most pious and god-fearing of mankind, and celebrated the most numerous and magnificent festivals in honour of the gods. They might be pious and god-fearing, for their resources allowed of it, and they realized the advantages of piety when they feasted on the sacrificial meats. What they offered to the gods, they themselves enjoyed, and they knew very well that the power of their Empire provided them with the possibility of expressing such piety towards their deities. At the great feasts at which their allies were present, they could bask in the sunshine of their power, when the grown-up sons of those who had fallen in war on behalf of the State were equipped with armour, or when the surplus funds of the public treasury, talent after talent, were carried across the orchestra of the Theatre of Dionysos and the allies brought their tribute. To the Great Panathenaia the smaller towns in Attica contributed victims and the allies suits of armour as well. The State soon discovered that it could make material profit out of cult. The hides of the many victims were sold for the benefit of the treasury and brought in a substantial revenue; but in Greece they did not go so far as the cities of Asia Minor, which auctioned their priesthoods to the highest bidder, for the priests received salaries consisting of certain fees for every sacrifice, and certain parts of the victims which fell to their share. The cult was secularized, for it was run on business lines.

It is not surprising that the average man in Athens was pious and would not allow criticism of the gods who gave him his Empire and on whose behalf such splendid festivals were celebrated. To this must be added a remnant of the ancient faith, but it was rather the minor deities and the heroes than the great gods of the State who were approached with pious reverence, for the former lay nearer to the heart of the people and there was more belief in their intervention in the life of the individual. Anyone might need the help of a god, and the victorious progress of Asklepios soon began. The Athenian man in the street forgot the lesson which the Pythia inculcated in the case of the rich Thessalian and the poor man of Hermione, if he had ever learned it. It did not concern him, for he was a poor man, a humble member of society who did not feel responsible for its defects, although he gladly took his share of the advantages which it offered as a not undeserved reward. The generality never does have a remorse of conscience; we do not speak of its contrition, but at most of a change in its opinion. In that age much was said about the overweening pride of mankind, its *hybris*, and the vengeance of the gods, *nemesis*, which struck down the proud, but the idea never occurred to them that a whole people may become guilty of such pride and be visited by *nemesis*. For indeed the gods and the State were one; finally the people, Demos, was personified and Democracy also had a cult. It is true that patriotism in that age could find expression only in religion, but it robbed religion of its proper and indwelling value; it became an apanage of patriotism, and the individual's piety had but a narrowly restricted place in this collective and patriotic worship.

It should also be noted that the Athenians tried to exploit religion to get a political confirmation of their leading position. About the year 448 B.C., they invited the Greek States to a congress at Athens to deliberate on the restoration of the temples destroyed by the Persians and on the offerings which the Greeks had vowed to the gods during the war of liberation. The egoistic purpose betrayed itself in an item which was included in the programme, a discussion of the means for giving all Greeks the use of the sea in time of peace. As this was manifestly aimed at strengthening the power of Athens at sea, the congress was shipwrecked upon the opposition of the Greek States to the project, and the Athenians built their own temples. Thus they did their duty by the gods and at the same time demonstrated, as the tyrants had done in their day, the power and glory of their State. Some time after, the Athenians tried to persuade the Greek States to join together around the Eleusinian Mysteries by paying tithes to the goddesses of Eleusis. The starting-point was well chosen, for it emphasized the position of Athens as the cradle of civilized and ethical life, but the cult of the Mysteries and the hopes of immortality were not yet strong enough to bridge over the political differences. Greek religion had lost its power of promoting unity, which might have served as a foundation for a confederacy of the many little States. This is made especially plain by the fact that the Delphic oracle lost its leading position; its authority was on the wane as religious belief grew weaker, and it could no longer keep above the contentions of political interests. In the Peloponnesian War it openly sided with the enemies of secularist Athens.

2. INDIVIDUALISTIC RELIGION

The concluding decades of the fifth century saw individualism force its way into Greek thought. The period is rightly styled an age of enlightenment, for the movement was wholly intellectualist and secular, and directed harsh criticism against religion, a matter to which we shall soon come; but it was inevitable that the newly awakened individualism should leave its mark on religion as elsewhere, although, by reason of the secular and anti-religious character of the new ideas, they started no new religious movements, as had been the case in the archaic period when the needs of individual religion took upon themselves ecstatic or mystical forms and their adherents organized themselves into groups, for religious zealots always look for companions and the support of brethren. The Orphics had a certain tendency to sectarianism and the Pythagoreans formed a brotherhood which drew a sharp line between itself and the surrounding world.

A trace of the influence of individualism on religion can, perhaps, be found in the numerous pictures, mostly on vases, which treat subjects from the Eleusinian Mysteries. At the end of the sixth and beginning of the following century, the central figure is Triptolemos, who by order of Demeter spread agriculture all over the world, whereby mankind left its bestial mode of life and learned the blessings of civilization, law, and justice. The claim of Athens to be the cradle of civilization rested as much on this universally accepted myth as on her pioneer contributions to philosophy, literature, and art. After the middle of the fifth century Triptolemos is no longer the central figure, and in place of him it is preferred to represent scenes of initiation into the mysteries in mythical disguise. It is reasonable to conjecture that the reason for this was the expectation of a blessed life beyond the grave which the initiated entertained. The pictures allude to what each one of the initiated hoped for himself; the thought of the civilizing mission of the cult and the hero of Eleusis for the good of mankind recedes into the background.

Just within the period of enlightenment falls the vigorous spread of the cult of Asklepios, the god of healing. His fame overstepped State frontiers, and branches of his worship were founded in many places, Attica, Delphoi, and Pergamon, and in the year 420 B.C. Asklepios was introduced into Athens, received by the poet Sophokles, and given a sanctuary on the south slope of the Akropolis, from which come many votive reliefs. At the beginning of the following century, monumental buildings were erected at his principal place of worship, Epidauros; a temple decorated with sculptures by the foremost artists of the day, the theatre, whose auditorium is the grandest and best-preserved in existence, a famous circular building, and many others. The costs were very heavy and must have been met from the revenues coming in from the throngs of seekers after help who visited Epidauros. Asklepios is the gentle and merciful god who helps and comforts men in bodily distress and sickness. Of all the Greek gods, he was surrounded with the warmest devotion and affection, and he kept his popularity until he had to give way to Christian saints who took over his activities. For religious feeling he had the same importance as Our Lady of Lourdes or the Panaghía Evangelistria of Tenos in our days.

Genuine piety was never lacking, but, as has been observed more than once, among simple folk this was oftener directed to the little gods who were nearer their lives and hearts than to the great deities of the State. A moving example is that of a poor immigrant into Attica, Archedemos of Thera, who was, as he put it, 'seized by the Nymphs' (the word signifies 'mad'). Sometime in the fifth century he devoted his attention to a grotto at Vari on Mount Hymettos, decorated it, carved inscriptions on its walls, and planted a garden in front of it.

3. CRITICISM

Ideas of all periods poured into and met in Athens. The natural philosophy of Ionia came there a century or a century and a half after its commencement, in the person of Perikles' friend Anaxagoras. This was the first attempt to explain the universe, its origin, and the phenomena of nature by physical causes; to call it scientific is not too much, although its explanations were as yet naïve and imperfect. The moon was another world, perhaps inhabited, the sun a mass of white-hot stone, a solar eclipse took place when the moon shadowed the sun, lightning and thunder occurred when clouds collided, and if they were pierced, rain came down. What the Athenians thought of these revolutionary explanations we may hear in Aristophanes' comedy *The Clouds*, from which we may also gather what impression they made.

From the other end of the Greek world came the first sophists. The word *sophistes* means a wise man, one who has knowledge or understanding of something. The sophists understood and could teach the art of effective speech and argument. Their prominence depended on the practical needs of life. Anyone at all might be obliged to appear before a tribunal. If he accused anyone or had to defend himself against an accusation, he must so arrange his speech and set forth his argument as to convince the jury, whose numbers ran into hundreds. If he desired political power and influence in a democratic State, he must know how to speak so as to get the majority of the popular Assembly on his side. Antiquity understood better than we do that this art can be learned, and the sophists founded and developed it. That their teaching was timely and met a strongly felt want was made plain by the numbers of young men who flocked around the sophists and paid them heavy fees.

The great defect of the sophists was that they did not pay attention to the ethical point of view; this is how their name got the ugly sound which it has in our language. They were charged with proving that black was white, and not without cause, for that art was one of the results of their teaching, but the saying which is sometimes understood in that way means in fact to make the case which is the weaker appear the stronger. Now a case which is weak is not necessarily a bad one, but the ethical standpoint is left out of account; it is merely a question of the technique of presentation. For that reason Plato despised the sophists and attacked them strongly.

The sophistical position was supported by the most philosophically minded of them, Protagoras, with a subjective philosophy. His famous fundamental axiom ran: Man is the measure of all things, both of the existence of the existent and the non-existence of the non-existent. I.e., everything is relative, everyone is right. As he put it, everything is true. The soul is nothing but the sense-perceptions. There is no common measure; what one thinks right is right for him, but may be wrong for another. This maxim set the individual free from the bonds of convention; every general standard was abolished, and the individual had the right to judge of everything according to his own understanding. On this was founded the egoism which Alkibiades,

Lysandros, and others translated into practice and which Kallikles preaches in the *Gorgias* of Plato.

The art of arguing and disputing was well suited to the Athenians' intellectualist temperament. It spread abroad, touched every relation of life, and most particularly concerned itself with the State (democracy was vigorously attacked and declared to be a confessed madness) and with religion. Against this the argument which natural philosophy furnished was also employed. Some have been surprised that Aristophanes in the *Clouds* confuses Sokrates with the sophists and makes him prove, by a physical explanation of thunder and rain, that Zeus does not exist; it is idiotic, it is declared, for a grown man to believe in him. This view of Aristophanes is right in so far as he uses Sokrates as a representative of the intelligentsia of the time, but it is wrong in confounding Sokrates with the sophists.

Both natural philosophy and sophistry were weapons in the intellectual arsenal of that day. The fundamental antithesis was that between *physis* and *nomos*. *Physis* is that which is naturally necessary, that which alone will stand examination and is recognized as inevitable. *Nomos* is commonly translated 'law', but it is law of human origin, what is established by man, custom, justice, religion; thus the idea is opposed to what we call natural law, which is *physis*. It was easy to observe that religion is a human invention. A century earlier Xenophanes had said that the Ethiopians conceive of their gods as black and flat-nosed, the Thracians of theirs as blue-eyed and red-haired. If oxen, horses, and lions could paint they would portray gods in their own likeness. Now the conclusion was drawn; man has created the gods in his own image, therefore the gods are a human invention, for they are different among different people.

The ethical arguments went deeper, for righteousness and good morals were demanded even of gods. It was an easy matter to muster the numerous objectionable myths which were told of gods. Xenophanes had already said that Homer

and Hesiod ascribed to the gods everything which was shameful and blameworthy among men, theft, adultery, and deceit.
This argument was now taken up with real fervour. Among
the many utterances in Euripides which deal with the gods'
shortcomings in justice and morality and their unmerciful
actions, we may cite the accusation of Apollo in his tragedy
Ion.

> Phoibos, a word with thee! What ails thee? Ravish
> A maid, betray her? What, beget a child,
> Then cast it forth and care not if it die?
> Nay, prithee; thou hast power, then follow virtue,
> Seeing that if a mortal man offends
> The gods are quick to punish. If for men
> Ye deities make laws, what justice is it
> When ye yourselves so lawless are adjudged?
> Should ye give satisfaction for your rapes
> (An idle thought, yet will I utter it),
> Thou and Poseidon, aye, and heaven's own King,
> Must strip your temples ere ye pay that fine.
> For still preferring before prudence lust,
> Ye haste to sin. Cease then to blame a man
> If he but imitate what gods commend;
> He does no wrong; the wrong is theirs who taught him.

Euripides sums up the criticism of the gods' ethical shortcomings in the familiar quotation 'if the gods do aught
shameful, they are no gods'. Cult underwent the same judgement. It is not right that an offender may take refuge at
the altars of the gods; he should be chased away, for the
hand which has committed an injustice ought not to touch
the gods. Earlier, Herakleitos had expressed himself most
pointedly. To cleanse oneself from blood with blood is like
washing off dirt with dirt, he says; to address the statues
of the gods is no better than to talk to a wall. But Herakleitos
lived in Ionia, and his obscure writings were not much known.
Now criticism broke loose in full force.

The finishing touch was given to the work by what seemed
a plausible explanation of how man discovered the gods and

came to believe in them. A starting-point was found in the transferred use of certain divine names in Homer; Aphrodite can mean sexual relations; pieces of meat are said to be held 'over Hephaistos', meaning over a fire. This started an explanation which Prodikos, one of the sophists, put forward. The ancients, he said, accounted as a god anything that was useful to man; the sun, the moon, rivers, springs. Therefore they called wine Dionysos, bread Demeter, water Poseidon, and fire Hephaistos. The nature of Greek gods did indeed give some show of justification to such an opinion. The author of the atomic theory, Demokritos the philosopher, drew attention to sudden and incalculable natural phenomena, lightning and thunder, comets, eclipses of the sun and moon. The maxim that fear gave birth to belief in gods had a long life.

Another method of explanation looked for the origin of both religion and justice in the development of human society. One of the disciples of the sophists, Kritias, best known as being the worst of the Thirty Tyrants who set up a régime of terror after the fall of Athens, wrote a play entitled *Sisyphos*, of which a long fragment is preserved treating of that very theme. Like Hesiod, he supposes that men originally lived like the wild beasts, without law or justice. To end the reign of war of all against all, they decided to establish rules of justice, *nomoi*, but as people continued still to act unjustly in secret, a wise man invented the gods to strike fear into the unjust if they secretly thought, said, or did anything unrighteous. This sage taught that an imperishable, divine being sees and hears everything. He thus 'obscured the truth with a false tale'. To awe mankind, he placed his gods in the place whence come those phenomena which both arouse fear and benefit us, lightning, thunder, sunshine, and rain. Thus he kept lawlessness within bounds. Kritias degraded the gods to a secret police who were so cleverly contrived that they could perceive the innermost thought of mankind. He thus combined Prodikos' views with the theories of the natural philosophers, for their explanations were concerned precisely with the origin of thunder and rain.

Unbelief spread among the educated. Xenophon in his *Memorabilia of Sokrates* shows us a young man who neither offered sacrifices nor consulted diviners, and was contemptuous of those who did so; Sokrates tries to convert him with the teleological proof of the existence of God. Sheer blasphemy was not lacking. Kinesias the poet gathered a Godless Club about him, whose members scoffed at the gods and at morality. Thucydides rejects everything supernatural from his historical narrative and mentions omens and oracles merely for their effect upon popular feeling. Plato informs us that in his day some believed that there were no gods, others that they did not concern themselves with mankind, others again that they could be influenced by sacrifices and prayers. The last was the popular belief. The attitude of the orators in the first half of the fourth century B.C. is significant; they respect the State religion, but at the same time scepticism shows itself in discreet phraseology and shows that fundamentally they shared the general unbelief.

Good Athenians believed that they believed in their gods, but the belief was beginning to fade. There are burlesque myths, but no one who has an atom of real belief treats gods as Aristophanes does. Dionysos, in the *Frogs*, appears as a cowardly youngster who is threatened with a beating by his own slave. The birds found a city which blockades the gods from their amorous adventures and shuts off the supply of sacrificial smoke, so that they are starved into surrender. When Plutos, the god of wealth, whom Zeus had blinded through jealousy, recovers his sight, no one offers any more sacrifices. Aristophanes waged war against the sophists, but he was a child of his age and knew what he could offer his public; and since the world of the gods provided him with profitable themes for his Gilbertian fantasies, he never noticed that he was giving the ancient pieties a slap in the face.

Belief in the gods had faded, but was not extinguished. If the fun went too far, it could blaze up into religious hysteria, as at the departure of the hazardous expedition against Syracuse and the notorious prosecutions which followed in connexion with the mutilation of the Hermai, in 415 B.C. To these was added an indictment of Alkibiades for profaning the Eleusinian Mysteries, but its political foundation was glaringly apparent, and was not wanting in the other religious indictments to which we shall come in the next section. Divination kept its hold over the popular mind, even over many who shared the education of that time. A noteworthy example is Xenophon. In his *Anabasis* he tells us again and again how he offered sacrifice and consulted diviners before every enterprise, and how he was guided by signs and omens. Of genuine religious thought or feeling there is not much in him save for worn-out phrases; but he very seldom mentions Tyche.

The old gods had been overthrown by criticism; they continued to exist only in public policy and in the minds of the simple and credulous, whom the discussions of their time passed by. The criticism of the gods' arbitrary conduct and their offences against justice and morality had done its work. Since the gods did not satisfy the demand that righteousness should be upheld, that they should be an expression and an embodiment of divine laws, they were set aside. Man has always contemplated deity and its activities in Nature; this was the basis of the old nature-worship and to this recourse was had in a form reshaped by philosophy. If the arbitrariness of the nature-gods had shaken belief in them, gods who followed immutable laws were discovered in the heavenly bodies; in their obedience to law was seen a proof of their divinity. In his old age, Plato found the true gods there. Thus a seed was sown which was to grow up into a tree that overshadowed the world, astrology.

4. CONFLICT

The same age which saw the ancient religion fall a victim
to criticism and lose its controlling power is also the age
of the notorious religious indictments. They usually had a
political basis, whether as a means for securing power in
political contests or, occasionally, for defending threatened
public morality as well. The notion which to us seems the
obvious one, that they were attempts to put down hetero-
dox thinkers with the help of the power of the State, in
other words heresy-hunts, misunderstands the true state of
affairs; freedom of thought and expression was absolute in
Athens. The accused were not charged with false doctrine
but with offences against the practices of cult. It has already
been pointed out that an offence against cult was punishable,
because it drew down the wrath of the gods not only against
the culprit but upon the whole people, unless the latter
atoned for the sin by punishing it. But we must add another
and less recognized point; there was a contest against divination, which had a strong hold on all the affairs of life.

Diviners were numerous and influential. The Athenian
State offered up no sacrifice without calling in a diviner; an
army was accompanied into the field by diviners, who made
sacrifices on every important occasion and interpreted the
omens; individuals went for advice to oracles and diviners.
The Athenian Assembly chose exegetes, interpreters, who
were specialists in the sacred rites, expounded them, and at
the same time were diviners. Many of these diviners were
highly respected men and influential politicians. It suffices
to mention one, Lampon, who for some decades after the
middle of the fifth century occupied a leading place in public
affairs; among other things he was credited with the foundation of the Athenian colony of Thurioi in south Italy.

Of this same Lampon a significant anecdote is told. A
ram with one horn in the middle of its forehead was brought
to Perikles. Lampon expounded the portent to mean that

of the two political rivals, Perikles and Thucydides (not the historian but a somewhat older statesman), that one would be victorious to whom the ram belonged. But Anaxagoras had the beast's skull opened and observed that its brain did not fill the cavity as usual, but was egg-shaped and connected with the root of the single horn, and that was why it had but one. Our informant adds that the people admired Anaxagoras much but Lampon still more when Thucydides was ostracized. Perikles, who adopted the modern ideas of his day, is said, on one occasion when an eclipse of the sun threatened to spread panic among the soldiers, to have held his cloak before a soldier's eyes and asked him if it was anything extraordinary that it was dark. A solar eclipse was one of the greatest portents. If portents depended on natural causes, then they were not sent by the gods, and the art of divination was nothing but a phantom of the mind.

The diviners saw what was going on, and it was but natural that they in particular came forward to champion their threatened art and the old religion in which divination played so important a role. The first indictment for impiety was directed against Perikles' friend, the natural philosopher Anaxagoras. Like the accusation of Perikles' mistress Aspasia, it was an attempt to undermine his leading position in public affairs. His rival Thucydides and the diviner Diopeithes seem to have co-operated in the indictment. By way of leading up to it, Diopeithes put a motion through the Assembly allowing indictments of any who did not believe in divine occurrences (*ta theia*), and taught concerning events in the upper air. The wording makes it plain that Diopeithes was thinking of divination in particular, for signs in heaven and in the air played a very prominent part in that.

During the preparations for the expedition against Syracuse in 415 B.C., feverish excitement prevailed in Athens. Warm contentions had taken place in the Assembly about this enterprise, whose leading advocate was Alkibiades, and everyone knew how venturesome and far-reaching his plans were. When, shortly before the fleet sailed, the herms which stood before the houses were found one morning to be mutilated (probably by drunken or unruly young men), the anxiety broke out in a religious panic; what had happened was both an offence against religion and an omen which foreboded evil. Alkibiades, whose overweening character was notorious, fell under suspicion, and his political opponents made the very most of their opportunity. They added an indictment for profaning the Eleusinian Mysteries. 'Profanation' is, however, not a fully adequate expression of the content of the indictment. A case which concerned these mysteries was tried before a special court, composed of initiates. Their rites must not be made public nor imitated, and it was precisely this latter offence with which Alkibiades was charged. About the same time, the same accusation was levelled against the most notorious atheist in antiquity, Diagoras of Melos, on whose head the Athenians set a high price. The Eleusinian cult was a particularly tender point, not only by reason of the sanctity with which it was surrounded, but also because it, if anything could, aroused genuine religious emotions.

The feeling of the Athenians at this time was described a little way back as hysterical. It would have been remarkable if their anger had not been directed against those who were always considered the authors of destructive criticism of religion, morality, and the State, also of the young men's self-will—the sophists. Old Protagoras was included in the condemnation and banished from Athens, for he was not an Athenian citizen, his native place being Abdera, and died on his way to Sicily; his writings were publicly burned in the market-place of Athens. According to our accounts, the reason for his banishment was the opening words of one of his books: 'Concerning the gods, I have no means of knowing whether they exist or not, for there are many hindrances to such knowledge, the obscurity of the matter and the shortness of human life.' Incidentally, this remark is very cautiously worded; Euripides, who put much more emphatic utterances into the mouths of his characters, was not molested. Protagoras fell a victim to the general ill will aroused by the sophists' rationalist practices.

It is from the same point of view that we must deal with the most notorious of these indictments, that which led to the death of Sokrates in 399 B.C. In his defence of him Plato mentions the popular accusations of which Aristophanes had been the spokesman in his comedy, *The Clouds*.

There is one Sokrates, a sophist (*sophòs anér*), a researcher into things in the sky and a discoverer of what lies under the earth, one who can make the weaker case appear the stronger.

Those who hear this suppose, Sokrates adds, that they who busy themselves with such researches are also disbelievers in the gods. The formal accusation was that Sokrates was guilty of corrupting the young and that he did not recognize (*ou nomízei*) the gods whom the State recognized but introduced new supernatural powers (*daimonia*). In the last word there was possibly an allusion to Sokrates' famous *daimonion*, an inward voice which sometimes spoke to warn him against an action. The word *nomízei* is hard to render correctly; it means to make a custom of something, especially something ordained by law; it could at a pinch mean that Sokrates alleged there are other gods than those recognized by the State, but to render it 'believe in' is to import a shade of meaning which does not belong. The accusers had chosen their wording so as to keep to the formal legal grounds which were always appealed to, but the question is if they could have done so in good faith; no real assumption of the sort was possible. The kernel of the matter was the reaction against the destructive activity of the sophists, with whom common opinion confused Sokrates.

The popular imputations against Sokrates included both natural philosophy and sophistry. The reference to 'what lies beneath the earth' must have alluded to the belief in the underworld and the punishments there, which at that period was by no means dead. Demokritos protested against it:

Some men, who do not know that the human organism dissolves (at death) and are conscious of their ill-doing in life, suffer all their days from disturbances and fears, inventing lying fables of the time after death.

Protagoras had written a book on the things in Hades. In the introduction to his work on the State, Plato represents old Kephalos as saying that when death draws near, a man who formerly gave no thought to such matters is seized with fear about the myths of the punishment of evil-doers in the underworld, which once he laughed at, and casts about to see if he has wronged anyone, and if he has many wrong-doings on his conscience he is filled with fear, has bad dreams, and forebodes the worst.

The accusation of Sokrates had a political background like the rest. It took place four years after the restoration of the democracy at Athens, following on the crushing defeat with which the Peloponnesian War ended and the terroristic government of the Thirty Tyrants, which led to civil war. All good powers must combine to give the wounded and torn State quiet and a possibility of convalescence, and it is un-mistakable that an honest attempt in that direction was made. The general opinion prevailed that the sophists, who made out that black was white and adopted the system of explain-ing things by natural philosophy, were the very root and ground of the breaking up of law and the young men's itch for disputation and their self-will. Sokrates' accusers were respectable citizens, who wanted to serve the community by restoring discipline and order. To them, Sokrates, with his everlasting discussions of everything with everybody and his provoking way of proving to them that they knew nothing, with his following of enthusiastic young disciples, was simply a sophist and a misleader of youth. Their tragic error was that they confused the conqueror of the sophists with the sophists themselves. We can understand that, but not excuse it.

Once religious indictments got under way it was possible for them to be inspired by personal spite, and that happened in the fourth century in the suits brought against, for instance, the famous courtesan Phryne and against Aristotle, who had been Alexander the Great's tutor. When the hatred of Macedonia broke out in Athens on receipt of the news that Alexander was dead, an accusation of impiety was brought against Aristotle, who retired to Chalkis in Euboia and died there shortly after. These indictments have but little interest in the present context; our aim has been to illustrate the unprofitable reaction against the criticism of religion and the blending of political motives with it.

5. THE EARLIER HELLENISTIC PERIOD

Greek religion passed through two great crises. The one, which led to the break-up of the old religious sentiment, began about a century after the new epoch in the national life which was brought about by averting the danger which threatened from the Oriental world-monarchy and exalted Athens to the position of a great power at sea and in the intellectual sphere. The second crisis, the conversion to credulity in matters of religion, began approximately a century after the world-conquest of Alexander the Great, which laid the East open to the Greeks and put the material and intellectual conditions of their life on a new foundation, developed beyond anything they had heard of. We shall soon come to the conditions leading to this change, but first something must be said of the religious position in the earlier Hellenistic period, the century immediately following the death of Alexander the Great. It need hardly be observed that, here as always, the distinction is not sharp; the old ideas survived for a long time, and the new ones worked their way forward only little by little.

From the religious point of view, the first century of the

Hellenistic period was a continuation of the previous age, although it also shows a marked characteristic, which was due to the fact that a new world had been opened for the Greeks. Their horizon had widened; their living-room extended to the cataracts of the Nile on the southern border of Egypt and eastward to the frontiers of India. Unguessed-of possibilities offered themselves for the enterprising and lucky. Alexander's generals won kingdoms, their assistants got power and wealth, many others found competences and importance from the exploitation of the conquered territories. Everyone was the maker of his own fortune, even people in quite humble positions, soldiers, merchants, engineers, artisans. It was an age of unheard-of expansion of power. Technical skill and specialist knowledge never in all antiquity celebrated such triumphs or took such a dominant position as in that century.

An age of materialistic leanings, which believes in its own power, has not much time to spare for religion, to which it grants only what outward circumstances demand. The new cult which arose, the worship of the kings, had its origins in Greece, where the custom had come in some time before of giving divine honours to those in power; in the last analysis it was irreligious, a glorification of naked force, and from the political point of view it was a means of holding together the heterogeneous population of the realm. A common civil law, which could have done the same, was wanting, and the only bond of union was the person of the monarch.

Such an age as that is likely to witness great and sudden alterations; a man could climb quickly to the height of fortune, but fall again as quickly. Formerly, the gods were credited with originating men's lot; the process of levelling was their work, for they struck down those who climbed too high. But the old notion of *hybris*, of over-much pride, disappeared, overwhelmed by consciousness of their own strength, and with it vanished the conception of equalizing justice, although the idea of retributive vengeance did not die out. The thought could not quite be got rid of that a higher power lay behind the events and exalted a man or cast him down. The age found that power in Tyche—Fortune, Fate, or, for the fortunate, Good Luck. Tyche is the last stage in the secularizing of religion in its conceptions of the powers which govern the universe and the destinies of man. The comedian Philemon puts the thought into most pointed words:

> In Tyche we have no deity, no, no! but what happens of itself (*to autómaton*) to each of us, that we call Tyche.

Tyche can quite simply and objectively signify the course of events, for instance in the great historian Polybios, who made it his aim to show the causal connexion of historical facts, in other words, to explain them and understand them from a rational standpoint. But occasionally even Polybios cannot get clear of the popular conception and uses its expressions. Tyche brings about great changes and plays with men as with little children; she is deceitful and incalculable, she loves to turn human reckonings upside-down. New Comedy has much to say of Tyche; she is blind and unhappy, unjust and senseless, she does three things badly for one well, she changes from day to day, she makes the rich poor, foresight and good council are of no avail against her. The feeling, however, that Tyche was a divine power had not been lost. A fragment of Menander says:

> Whether Tyche is a divine afflatus or an intelligence (*nous*), it is she who guides all things and turns them about and saves them, whereas human foresight is nothingness and idle chatter.

However, men could not get rid of the thought that there are gods who govern their destinies. The forms of religion were so influential that they forced even Tyche into their sphere. Tyche was personified and became a goddess, with the natural result that her bestowal of good luck was emphasized. She received temples and statues, which showed her holding a steering-oar, a cornucopia, and sometimes with a mural crown on her head, for she became the tutelary goddess of cities. She was given an altar in domestic worship, but in New Comedy she does not appear as a goddess with a cult.

People in Hellenistic times had lost the support and comfort which a living religious faith can give against the blows of fortune and the unwelcome events of life. They were like men driven hither and thither at sea without a rudder, at the mercy of the waves. Criticism and unbelief had wrenched the tiller from the hands of the gods, but philosophy offered men a rudder and prompted them to steer their ship along a course which aimed at freeing them from the blows and arbitrariness of Tyche. It offered them deliverance from destiny, but it was a deliverance which they must gain by their own power. But their powers were feeble and, then as always, men needed support, aid, and comfort. Philosophers took over the cure of souls.

The two philosophical schools which arose at the beginning of the Hellenistic age and were dominant through and beyond it, Stoicism and Epicureanism, both made ethics their chief business; both appealed to the individual and had little attention to spare for human society; Stoicism preached cosmopolitanism. It was a strong individualism, which advised all to follow the path of duty and meet the blows of fate manfully; it became the lode-star of many a public man. Epicurus found happiness in pleasure, or rather in a balance between pleasure and pain in which the former outweighed the latter. He set a high value on friendship and advised men to live in quiet, unnoticed, for thus they were least exposed to the blows of fate. Epicureanism was a weak individualism.

Philosophy took the place of religion as the comforter and guide of humanity, and there is plenty of evidence that it was able to give mankind power to stand up to the storms of life; but it was a view of life fit only for the educated, who thought seriously about existence, not for the great mass of humanity, which needed, not philosophical maxims, but a firm, concrete belief.

Philosophy could not avoid including religion in its investigations, since that had such great importance for the thought and actions of humanity. Epicurus did not deny the existence of the gods, but he degraded them to *rois fainéants*, living in the spaces between the universes, without passions, inaccessible, occupied in contemplating their own happiness and perfection. The Stoic god was immanent in the world; he was intelligence, identified with fire, which penetrated everything and was to be found in everything, even in the smallest particle. The world was governed by him according to a rational plan, and it was man's duty to subordinate himself to this plan, to Providence, and live in conformity with it. Sometimes this god is given a personal colouring, for instance in Kleanthes' famous hymn, where he is called Zeus, but in spite of all there is a rather icy coldness brooding over what he says and such warmth as it possesses originates in the old conceptions of the highest god of the Greeks. Religious sentiment increased among the Stoics as time went on, becoming more prominent as their ethics lost their defiant sharpness and became more human; Epiktetos' book is still one of the greatest works of edification of all time. But it belongs to a much later period than the one of which we are now speaking.

To judge by its principles, Stoicism ought not to have had much room for religion and religious belief, but it showed remarkable aptitude for incorporating religious phenomena in its system and explaining them. Like Epicureanism, it suffered from an antiquated explanation of the universe, and when Poseidonios, in the last century B.C., worked the new results of science into his system, it fell straight into the arms of the doctrine of magical force and of astrology. Philosophy took up and developed the old explanations of the origins of the belief in gods, but the doctrine which goes by the name of Euhemeros was much more important. From of old, mythology had been treated as the most ancient history, and it was a bold but logical step to transfer this treatment from mythical heroes to mythical gods, and to put forward the view that the gods were powerful kings of pre-historic times who by their exploits had contrived to get divine honours for themselves. This doctrine put a full stop to the old belief in gods, if these were nothing but long-dead men who had been worshipped as gods in their life-time and after their death, like Hellenistic kings. Euhemeros' book circulated widely, and was one of the first to be translated into Latin.

On the other hand, one of Plato's successors, Xenokrates, developed a doctrine which was to have a fatal influence in later days, in that it joined hands with the lower forms of popular belief. Xenokrates was a man inclined towards an ascetic life and took offence at the many cult-practices which were obviously at variance with humanity and ethics—unlucky days, festivals which were celebrated with fasting, mourning usages, or occasionally unclean speech. As he could not conceive that men should honour gods in this way, he took up certain hints in Plato concerning daimones as intermediate beings between gods and men and built on to them. The daimones have their abode in the air, under the moon; their nature is a combination of the divine, the spiritual, and the corporeal; they know pleasure and pain, and some of them are good, some bad. To the bad daimones he ascribed the objectionable cult-practices mentioned above. This doctrine became extraordinarily popular. If Xeno-krates believed that he had thereby delivered the gods from scandal, the real result was that the gods were degraded. For, even though they formed the highest class of super-natural beings, the medium through which they made con-nexion with mankind was the daimones, among whom were evil beings as well as good. Christianity drew the conclusion when it counted the old gods among the evil daimones.

Aristotle's successor Theophrastos displayed the same

desire to rid religion of unedifying practices in a work which he wrote on piety. He declared the central rite of paganism, animal sacrifice, to be unjust and impious, for one ought not to deprive anything, not even a beast, of the most precious of all gifts, life. Offerings should be made only of the fruits of the earth, and the gods value the pure heart of the sacrificer more than the number and costliness of the sacrifices. The defect was that criticism was directed against the conventional religion, and nothing more; Theophrastos was not a religious reformer, to replace what he attacked by something better. His argument also was used in late times for polemic against paganism.

The search for a deeper piety arising from a pious disposition is unmistakable in the two last-named philosophers, and their search made itself felt in wider circles, to which sundry epigrams and inscriptions testify, for they call for not only pure hands but also a pure heart in those who sacrifice or who visit a sanctuary. This is a deepening of religious ethics, but as yet this tendency was of no great consequence; later the other religions, especially Christianity, profited by it.

Unbelief spread widely during the earlier Hellenistic period, and downright blasphemy was not lacking. The explanations of the origin of the gods supported unbelief. The philosophers divided theology into three kinds: the physical, which was the explanation of the gods offered by natural philosophy; the mythical, that is, the accounts given of them by myths and in poetry; finally the political, which is the arrangements made by each State regarding the gods and their cult. This last is a creation of politicians, whose significance Polybios explains in the following manner:

If it were possible to get together a commonwealth of wise men, there might be no need for anything of this kind; but since every mob is unstable and full of lawless desires, unreasonable anger and violent rage, the only course remaining is to restrain the multitude with indefinite fears and such-like stage-machinery. Therefore I think that the ancients, when they introduced among the many these ideas concerning gods and conceptions of what happens in the under-world, were not acting aimlessly nor without meaning; it is much more the moderns whose action in trying to cast out such notions is aimless and unreasonable.

It is the same doctrine which Kritias had taught, but the times had changed. Whereas the age of enlightenment sought to show that belief in the gods was false, and so to uproot it, statesmen now took up the position that, while certainly an illusion, it ought to be retained and upheld to keep the rest-less, passionate, and unreasonable masses in order. One could hardly degrade religion more than that.

Although cult continued along the old lines, although voices were heard crying for a deepening of religion, yet religious feeling never was lower than when the Hellenistic period began. It was replaced by belief in one's own power and trust in Tyche, and, among the educated, by the philo-sophers' doctrine concerning life. For the common people there remained cult and the lower forms of religion, supple-mented by superstition, which usually increases in a time when the old religions are falling. The ground was cleared and a new structure must arise to make a place for religious feeling; a new religion must replace the old one which had withered away.

III

REBUILDING

THE reason for the long duration of the new crisis in the history of Greek religion (its first signs appeared about 200 B.C. and it did not really come to an end till half a millennium later, with the victory of Christianity) is that it was no longer a matter of pulling down but of building up something new from the foundations, something which should be more appropriate to the needs of the age and of humanity. During this long period, moreover, there occurred considerable changes in both intellectual and social life, which were not without their influence on religious development.

The beginning of this crisis coincides with the period in which the internal collapse and outward impotence of the Hellenistic States became apparent. Ptolemy IV, king of Egypt, defeated Antiochos III of Syria at Raphia in 217 B.C., but had little joy of his victory, which he won with the help of Egyptian troops armed and drilled after the Macedonian fashion; for the Egyptians' self-esteem and their enmity towards their Greek rulers increased and led to disquiet and uprisings, which the government was never able to keep down. The political connexions between Egypt and Greece came to an end. Antiochos III was crushingly defeated by the Romans at Magnesia in Asia Minor in 190 B.C.; his empire was curtailed and condemned to impotence, and after a while lost Babylonia to the Parthians. The Romans became masters of the eastern Mediterranean and pursued a policy which deliberately weakened the Hellenistic kingdoms, so as to turn them into vassal States with no will of their own; after the passage of a century or so they were incorporated as provinces into the Roman Empire.

Both Egypt and Syria were disquieted by the repeated

occurrence of violent contests between pretenders to the throne, which contributed largely to their downfall, but still more unfortunate was the corruption of the government, which undermined the prosperity of the people and the economy of the State. The useful arts shared the general collapse, which deprived them of the prerequisites for their existence; the flourishing condition of the special sciences which depended upon the generous support of the Egyptian kings came to an end. The consciousness of power which had been the hall-mark of the beginning of the Hellenistic period changed to helpless resignation.

By that time the Greeks had lived with and among the Eastern people for over a century. The Orientals were much more numerous than they; they surrounded their cities and communities like a sea around small islands, and lived even in the Greek communities. Common life led to a crossing of blood and of ideas. Many Greeks in humble circumstances intermarried with native women, and from these marriages, as also from the numerous casual relationships, there sprang up a mixed race which had no firm foothold with either its fathers' or its mothers' people, but shared in the aptitudes and conceptions of both. What these half-breeds meant for the blending of Greek and Oriental, to which latter Egypt also belongs, we cannot know, but they must have made a very considerable contribution to it.

Quite apart from this the Greeks were profoundly influenced by the Eastern world of ideas. They had long admired the wisdom of the Orient, and this admiration paved the way for appropriating it as a result of the continuous and close association with the Eastern people. The focal points of Greek education had moved to countries with a foreign population, especially to Alexandria, which sometimes gives the epoch its name, the Alexandrian Age, Antioch, a city of which we hear less, and Pergamon, which was indeed a Greek city but stood in Asia Minor and had a very mixed population. Finally philosophy, for which freedom of thought and expression was a vital necessity, disdained royal patronage and took up its abode in Greece, at Athens and Rhodes.

The Greeks took their gods and their worship with them, practising their cults and reverencing their deities even on foreign soil, that is to say, the great, universal gods; the local godlings and the heroes, who were so important for the common people, could not be transplanted. The Greeks founded new cities in the East, provided them with the usual equipment of gods and cults, but the citizens of these cities were descended from many different Greek States; they lacked the old fundamental prerequisite for religion, their city and its gods had not grown together into a unity, for such an inner connexion is the work of centuries during which gods and men live together. It is significant that Tyche became the tutelary goddess of the new cities. The old religion was buttressed by the routine of worship and by the conceptions of the gods formed by literature and art. These were inculcated in the schools, where Homer was the first reading-book, and fortified by the reading of literature. The school was the institution which kept Greek nationality, education, and ideas on their feet in foreign countries.

Greeks always kept to the principle of honouring and worshipping the gods of the country to which they had come. Since they now lived permanently abroad, these gods offered a substitute for the local deities which they had worshipped at home but could not take with them when they emigrated. Thus the Egyptian and Oriental gods took on a real importance for them, and were no longer simply foreign peoples' deities. The Oriental gods made their way into Greece also, above all those of Egypt, who became very popular. The half-Egyptian, half-Greek cult of Sarapis was certainly promoted by the attempts of the kings of Egypt to advance their interests in Greece, and in his train came Isis, whose cult spread very widely and who found many temples and adherents.

Theocrasy, the blending together of the gods of different

peoples, which depended upon the Greek opinion that the name of a god could and should be translated like any other word in the language, increased more and more; but still more important was the circumstance that the Greek gods were no longer sufficient for the religious demands which the violent enlargement of life and the world brought with it. They were national, bound up with the land and its people, and could not take root in foreign soil. What was wanted now was a god or gods to correspond to the widened horizon of the world, a god who ruled over everything and everyone, not merely over Greece or Egypt or some other country. Neither the Greek nor the Egyptian gods could satisfy this imperative demand, although Isis made some attempt at it.

The net result is, then, that neither the Greek nor the foreign deities answered to the genuine religious demands of the time; theocrasy was insufficient, the new must slowly work its way out from the existing presuppositions, among which the influence of Oriental ideas upon the Greeks took a leading place. The old Greek religion belonged to the Greek nation, the new one which was growing up must embrace the whole world, and under the existing circumstances as we have described them it must arise from a combination of the Greek and the foreign, Oriental elements, which mutually affected and reshaped each other. It is therefore known as syncretism, combination of religions, but it was not a random combination but crystallized out around certain leading ideas.

Finally, we must direct attention to one of these guiding lines which was an often neglected but certainly important preliminary, science. The study of special sciences was intensified in a decisive manner after Aristotle, the real founder of empirical research, and got far beyond the older results, thanks to the contribution of the great Alexandrian researchers. At the date which is taken here as a point of departure, degeneration had already set in, but on the other hand scientific results had spread to wider circles and begun to filter down to the general public, to the extent and in the way that it could understand them. The old conceptions about the universe underwent a complete revolution.

2. THE NEW COSMOLOGY

Ideas of the constitution and arrangement of the universe to which the earth belongs, of which we ourselves are a tiny part and which our life in the last resort touches, have a decisive influence upon religious ideas, which the advance of natural science in modern times has fundamentally reshaped. No one who has the least knowledge of the results of geology can take the six days of creation in Genesis literally. At the end of last century, the doctrine of Evolution was much to the fore in the struggle between science and religion, and it left profound traces. Reference is still often made to the battle which was fought out in the seventeenth century, when the earth was torn from its place in the centre of the universe and became one of the planets, moving around the sun with the rest. It did no good when the Inquisition forced Galileo to recant the heliocentric system, for soon it passed into the general consciousness as something self-evident.

Earlier than either the present heliocentric or the old geocentric cosmology (the latter is here called new, because it was new in antiquity), there was another, still older, naïve picture, best known to us from Homer and mythology, but dominant throughout the classical period and possessed in common by the Greeks and all peoples in an archaic stage of culture. This primitive image of the universe was narrowly bounded and compactly joined. Earth was a flat disk, circular like the horizon, with water (Ocean) flowing around it, while the vault of heaven curved above and beneath was the underworld, the dark and dreary abode of the dead. This world had a low ceiling, for heaven was the place of clouds, from which lightnings come down and the rain descends. The heavenly bodies were seen and known, but no one inquired how far off they were, for no one distinguished between atmospheric and celestial phenomena.

In this cosmology the gods were close at hand and could intervene in their own persons; they were active in the air, the water, and on earth, where they lived in wood and field, in rivers and springs; even the great gods might be met with there, but otherwise it was supposed that, as Homer represents it, their dwelling-place was on the summit of a high mountain, Olympos, which was identified with the sky because clouds collect around mountain-tops and from them the lightning flashes and the rain pours down.

The second of the Ionian natural philosophers, Anaximandros, put forward in the middle of the sixth century B.C. the hypothesis, for so we must call his assumption, keeping in mind the knowledge available in his day, that the earth hung free in space, although he still kept a remnant of the old cosmology in that he conceived of it as a squat cylinder. Anaximandros arrived at his hypothesis by a process of logical reasoning. Since the stars move around the earth on circular paths, they must have a clear way underneath as well as above the earth; therefore the earth must hang free in space. What appears to us self-evident, because it is impressed upon us from childhood (it is true that most of us could not give a proof of it), was in those days unheard-of boldness. Could not anyone see that what hangs unsupported must fall? An earth hanging free must fall; no one asked where to.

It took about half a millennium before the new cosmology was generally recognized. Although astronomy had already made considerable progress by the time of Plato, this recognition did not come till the beginning of the Hellenistic epoch, when Aristotle collected the proofs of the spherical form of the earth and one of the great Alexandrian scientists, Eratosthenes, covered the globe with a network of degrees of latitude and longitude, by the help of which he gave the position of places and calculated the circumference. His method was to measure the distance from Alexandria to the

southern border of Egypt; then, by taking the sun's distance
from the zenith on a given day of the year at both spots,
he got the angular difference with the help of which the
circumference of the earth could be calculated. He came
out to a result which, though decidedly too large, yet was
amazingly good allowing for the imperfect means of measure-
ment at that date and certain defects in his preliminary
calculations.

Astronomy became the fashionable science in Hellenistic
times. No composition of that age gained such popularity
as Aratos' didactic poem on the starry heavens, none was so
thoroughly commented on nor so often rendered into Latin.
Mythology was enriched with a crowd of catasterisms, that
is, myths about the change of human beings or beasts into
stars; the heroes and heroines of these tales found a place in
the celestial vault which they still occupy. Astrology, which
founded its system upon the new cosmology, crowned the
work by impressing it upon the general public. We can form
a lively idea of what the public knew and thought in a discourse to which the rich but uneducated parvenu Trimalchio
treats his guests in Petronius' audacious society romance. It
begins:

'This 'ere sky, as the twelve gods lives in, it turns into twelve shapes,
and sometimes it's a ram' [he means the twelve signs of the Zodiac,
and proceeds to go through them all, concluding], 'an' Mother Earth
sits in the middle, round as a egg.'

At the beginning of the third century B.C., Aristarchos of
Samos put forward the view that the earth turns on its axis
and, with the other planets, revolves around the sun, and
that the sun is the central point of an infinite universe. He
found a follower in the astronomer Seleukos, concerning
whom we have unfortunately only slight information. It is
said that he proved the heliocentric system of the universe
and explained the tides by the attraction of the moon. It
did not matter so much in antiquity that the philosopher
Kleanthes attacked Aristarchos for impiety, the same accusa-

tion which was brought against Galileo; it was more important that the greatest astronomer and most exact observer among the ancients, Hipparchos of Nikaia, undervalued Aristarchos' theory, because the geocentric system fitted his observations as well as the heliocentric. In the then condition of science, Hipparchos is not to be blamed, for an old theory is not rejected until the new one shows its superiority by fitting the factual material better. Copernicus knew Aristarchos' theory; his merit is that he proved it by better means of research.

The old cosmology was shattered and the universe expanded dizzily. Earth occupied the centre, surrounded by the atmosphere, and around it turned the seven spheres of the heavenly bodies, that of the moon being the lowest, while the eighth and highest was the sphere of the fixed stars in which the Zodiac with its twelve signs, the path on which the heavenly bodies travelled, occupied the most important place. From the middle of the Hellenistic period at latest, these bodies were arranged on a scientific principle, that of their periods of revolution: Moon, Mercury, Venus, the Sun, Mars, Jupiter, Saturn; that is our order also, except that in place of the sun we put the earth with its satellite the moon. This order differed from the older Greek arrangement only in this, that the latter put the moon and sun first and made the other planets follow them. Now the sun was in the middle, flanked on either side by three planets like satellites, which he alternately drew towards him and repelled from him; he became the leader, the coryphaeus, for he led the choir of heaven, a genuinely Greek idea which conferred upon him the foremost place in the universe. Probably the ultimate reason for the dominant position ascribed to the sun was the feeling that he is the cause of all life on earth. The Stoics quite naturally discovered their fundamental cosmic principle, the fire which is also intelligence, in the sun. The foundations for a solar religion were thus laid.

On earth, to which the atmosphere belongs as clothes do to

a man, a continual change, a passing out of and coming into being, defect and imperfection bear sway; in the celestial spheres, on the contrary, there is an eternal, immutable obedience to law; for these spheres were divine, the heavenly bodies themselves being indeed visible gods. So Aristotle already established the fundamental distinction between the sublunary and superlunary worlds, that is, the regions respectively below and above the moon, the former being defective and perishable, the latter eternal, imperishable, and divine. Under the influence of Platonic thought this distinction was deepened, so that the mutable, perishable sublunary world became the inferior, even the abode of evil, while the imperishable and eternal superlunary region was the higher and divine. Since the earth was peopled by human beings, the superlunary region by gods, there appeared a gap which must be filled if the air was not to be left uninhabited. The answer was given in accordance with ancient popular belief; the air was the abode of souls and daimones, the mediators and intermediate beings between gods and men, who are active in that space.

The ancient mythical cosmogony, however, was not forgotten, and cosmogonies of other peoples, Phoenician, Babylonian, and Egyptian, are mentioned in Greek writers. Certain religious movements formed cosmogonies of their own, e.g. Hermetism. In the Hermetic treatise *Poimandres*, a scene of cosmogony is described. Everything became a glorious light, but soon there descended a horrible darkness which turned into boiling water from which there came up smoke as from a fire and an indescribable noise. Next was heard an inarticulate cry, which seemed the cry of light. Then came forth from the light an utterance to Nature, and fire sprang up from the moist element. The air followed the breath (*pneuma*) and rose up from the earth and water till it reached the fire, but earth and water remained combined with each other. This is the creation of the world from the four elements by the word of power; it is possible that this fantasy is coloured by Jewish influence. A yet more fantastic cosmogony with traces of astrology is to be found in another Hermetic writing, the *Kore Kosmou*. Such cosmogonies were confined to particular circles and exercised no great influence outside them, but they show the eagerness of religious sects to form a picture of the origin of the universe. The new scientific cosmology exercised a compelling power over men's thoughts, consciously or unconsciously; no one could neglect it.

The consequences which the new cosmology brought about for religious thought were profound and extensive; we will illustrate them in detail in the following pages, but here only one is to be touched upon which, although not the most important in itself, became decidedly significant. In the new scheme of the world, which put the earth hanging free in space, there was no room for the underworld, the realm of the dead under the surface of the earth. A writing of fairly early date which got itself included among Plato's works, the *Axiochos*, solves the problem by assigning the upper hemisphere to the celestial gods, the lower to those of the underworld, it being turned away from mankind. This is a last remnant of the old ideas and presupposes that the earth rests immovable in the middle of the universe; it became untenable as soon as it was known that it revolves on its axis. Equally incompatible was the attempt to transfer the underworld to the sky, which was done by giving to certain constellations in the southern heavens names borrowed from the myths of Hades. The old notion that the soul, when set free at death, mounts into the air and sometimes turns into a star was easier to combine with the new system of the universe. It found support in the Stoic doctrine that the soul is a spark of the world-fire and returns to it after death; and it developed in various ways.

The atmosphere became the first abode of the soul, and there it was punished and purified by being washed with rain, burned with fire, and agitated with wind, as the older

belief had made it be punished and purified in the underworld. The further fate of the soul was described by a
philosophical reshaping of an old belief, to be observed in
India also. When it has been purified it mounts up to the
moon and lives there until it suffers a second death in which
the intelligence is parted from the soul, as the soul parts from
the body in earthly death, and passes into the primary fire,
the sun. Under astrological influence another doctrine was
developed which fitted the new cosmology still better. The
soul mounts through the seven planetary spheres, in which
it loses the qualities and defects corresponding to the
astrological character of each planet, until, naked and pure,
it gains the eighth sphere. In the same way it is clad in its
qualities by the planets when it is sent from that sphere
down to earth in order to be incarnated in a human body.
None of these conceptions was popular except the simple
idea that the souls of the pious, after death, mount up to
heaven and gather around the throne of the Most High; the
old belief in the underworld maintained itself with extraordinary vigour.

A modern is inclined to suppose that since the earth was
the centre in the geocentric system, earth and earthly phenomena must also have occupied the centre of human conceptions. For, when a modern examines his cosmology, he feels
that he is but a grain of dust in the endless whirl of the
universe. However, this antithesis could not come about
until the geocentric and heliocentric systems were opposed
to one another, which opposition did not exist in antiquity,
as Aristarchos of Samos' hypothesis remained unnoticed.
Within the universe as he saw it, a man in antiquity likewise
perceived his own pettiness, but qualitatively, not quantita-
tively as we do. Man was a microcosm, a model of the
macrocosm, the universe, and like it he was divided into a
material and perishable part and a divine, spiritual and
imperishable. He felt himself like a prisoner, pent within the
bars of the earth and his body, and turned his gaze up to the

endless space of the celestial region, which the fetters of corporality prevented him from approaching.

3. POWER

Belief in the wonderful power which in many religions, e.g. that of Egypt, distinguishes the gods, and which sorcerers think they control to attain their ends, was as good as extinct in archaic Greek religion; what possibly remained of it was unintelligible survivals. Homer tries to explain divine intervention after a fashion intelligible to human reason; only the enemy's formidable god Apollo keeps something of the marvellous powers of deity. Sorcery existed, but the Greeks showed little liking for it and relegated it to the region of popular superstition and folk-medicine.

The Greeks had of course a concept of power and a word to denote it. Aristotle analysed the concept and distinguished between *dýnamis*, potential force, and *enérgeia*, force in action. When, however, these words occur later in a religious context, they generally are used without distinction. The science of the Hellenistic period took up the concept of power; for instance, it explained the fact that a lodestone can attract iron filings by its 'power'. A leading axiom in the physics of the Stoic philosophy was universal sympathy. The word 'sympathy' must not here be understood in the sense it has in modern languages, but in its proper Greek meaning, which is that if one thing is affected, another thing is also affected thereby. This sympathy is inherent in matter, not a quality separable from it. Poseidonios, the great renovator of Stoic philosophy in the last century B.C., singled out this idea of power and made it into a leading conception; his philosophy is dynamic, in contrast to the older Stoicism, which was static. He associated himself with the great expansion which the idea of power gained in his day.

The ancients, unlike modern science, could not distinguish between different kinds of force, any more than they could measure force; incidentally, one can hardly say they had a concept of force, but only a vague and indefinite notion of it. On the other hand, the ancients did not think of force, or power, in so abstract a way as modern science generally does, but pictured it as an effluence (*apórrhoia*) or a breath of wind (*pneuma, pnoé*) or the like. Plutarch speaks, in a physiological discussion, of the currents (*rheúmata*) from beasts, plants, the earth, the sea, stones, and metals, and in another place of effluences (*apórrhoiai*) from a marvellous plant. The latter word is exactly the same as is used to denote the influence of the stars on earthly things. Still more familiar in the religious vocabulary is the word which denotes a draught of air, a breath (*pnoé, pneuma, émpnoia*); this later lost its material meaning.

The concept of power, from its very indefiniteness, came from the very beginning perilously near the wonderful and miraculous, to which that age was much inclined, as is shown by a whole wealth of literature dealing with marvellous objects and phenomena. The 'power' became mysterious and occult.

The man who finally developed the idea in the direction of the occult and founded a pseudo-science which governed antiquity and the following age down to the gold-makers of the seventeenth century was an Egyptian named Bolos, of Mendes in the Delta, who flourished about 200 B.C. and is commonly called the Demokriteian; the founder of atomic physics came into an unearned notoriety as a representative of the doctrine of occult power. Bolos knew the Egyptian traditions and the old recipes for colouring metals, precious stones, and cloth which were preserved in the Egyptian temples, and treated of them in his work, which was written in Greek; from what is known of his activities generally, he must be considered the founder of alchemy. His most important writing had a double title, *Physikà dynamerá*, i.e. 'the forces in Nature' or *Perì sympatheiôn kai antipatheiôn*, 'concerning sympathies and antipathies', which words are to be understood in the sense already explained. 'Antipathy'

means that something is affected when something else is
affected, and thus came to mean simply aversion, antipathy
in the modern sense, although this 'antipathy' is a physical
force, and thus the word came to mean an averting force, a
healing power; an *antipathès* is a means of counteracting
something, a remedy, of that kind which found its most
widespread application in magic. Bolos in this work described
the sympathies and antipathies between beasts, plants, and
stones in alphabetical order. He was a very diligent writer,
who produced works on agriculture, medicine, magic,
miracles, astrology, divination, and sundry other matters;
the spirit of his productions has already been sufficiently
illustrated. He was much read and found many imitators,
while his posthumous influence extended right down to
modern times.

A fateful result of this literature was that by means of its
'physical' explanations it lent a show of justification to the
many marvellous things and the numerous popular superstitions which it took up and which tickled the taste of that age
for the miraculous and occult. The serious researches into
natural science of the earlier Hellenistic period were replaced
by an endeavour to seek out and display the mysterious and
marvellous powers of natural objects within the whole
compass of the organic and inorganic fields, their occult
properties and the sympathies and antipathies depending on
these, in all natural kingdoms. Human beings, the lower
animals, plants, stones, metals, were all conceived of as the
carriers of mysterious forces which had the power to cure
sickness and suffering and to procure men riches, good luck,
honour, and wonderful potencies.

To understand how it was possible that this sham science
succeeded and spread so rapidly, we must remember that
antiquity could not differentiate between natural and occult
potencies, all forces becoming more or less occult. It is
significant that the very word 'physical' (*physikós*) in later
times commonly meant an occult property or potency. Thus

we discover the remarkable phenomenon that Greek science at first and afterwards the pseudo-science which built upon it contributed mightily to breathe new life into the almost vanished idea of and belief in power in the religious sphere, which had a fatal effect on religious activities in late antiquity.

Towards the end of the Hellenistic age the gods no longer appeared in their own person to perform marvellous acts; what was called an epiphany, that is, an appearance, of a deity was a manifestation of their wonderful powers, their *dynámeis* or *enérgeiai*, or, as they are often styled in eulogies of their deeds, *aretai*, that is, virtues, great actions. The notion of the power of the gods found a connecting link in the physical explanation of the deities and the transferred use of their names. Gods were discovered, not in the phenomena of nature, but in the potencies which whatever was designated by the different names of gods could produce. The origin of the belief in gods was explained by certain effects which it seemed impossible to bring about otherwise than by reason of certain powers appearing in human shape and called gods. A Byzantine author says very justly,

You must know that the pagans (*Héllenes*, pagan Greeks) supposed that all that they saw possessed of power could not exercise that power without the superintendence of gods, and they called that which was possessed of power and its superintendent deity by the same name. Hence they used 'Hephaistos' to mean the fire which serves us and the superintendent of the arts which are active by means of fire.

Philon, who tried to combine Jewish orthodoxy with Greek philosophy, uses the word *dýnamis*, or power, in order to include under a single concept the properties and the actions of the Jewish God, which are found side by side with no connecting link, by representing them as active powers, intermediaries between God and the world, and now and then identifying them with the angels. Porphyry, in his treatise on images of the gods, always looks behind the gods themselves for the powers which the gods possess. An inscription from Lydia says 'one god in the heavens, the celestial Mên, the great power of the immortal God'. As, towards the end of paganism, those who did not reject polytheism tried to reconcile it with the monotheism which the higher conceptions of deity in that age demanded, they found the concept of power most convenient; for instance, all the various gods were represented as powers of the sun-god. In one of the Hermetic writings, Aion, the duration of the world, is called 'the power of God', and in the principal Hermetic treatise, the *Poimandres*, we find the final issue and crown of this development. When the soul in its ascent through the seven planetary spheres is stripped of its human powers, it approaches the eighth sphere equipped with its own power alone and joins those who are there in a hymn of praise to the Father. It hears the potencies above the eighth sphere praising God. They then arise in order to the Father and give themselves up to Him to become powers; and when they are powers, they are in God. This, the author concludes, is the good end for those who possess the highest enlightenment (*gnosis*), to become divine.

It need hardly be mentioned that this doctrine served to explain the wonderful effects which were ascribed to images of the gods and the numerous methods for predicting coming events. Even the philosopher Plotinos taught that though certainly the gods themselves did not take up their abode in images, yet their power did so, and one of his successors, Iamblichos, was of opinion that the ineffable power of the gods itself recognized their statues. By means of complicated ceremonies the attempt was made to call down the god's power into his image. We are informed concerning an Egyptian 'philosopher', Heraïskos, that he possessed the ability to tell 'living' from 'lifeless' images of gods. As soon as he beheld a 'living' image, his heart was filled with divine inspiration, his limbs and his soul were set in motion as if he were possessed by the god. If he experienced nothing of the kind, the image was 'lifeless' and lacked the divine potency (*epipnoia*). As for divination, it suffices to remember the saying of Iamblichos, that the divine powers are able to animate that which has no soul and set in motion that which cannot move, for instance pebbles, bits of wood, corn, or flour; he alludes to certain known methods by which the above-named things were used for divining.

With this we have reached superstition. The wheel has come full circle and we are back at the idea which was mentioned at the beginning, magic and belief in sorcery, the many amulets which nearly everybody wore as a means of protection against ill or as mascots. Such things have always existed, but in late antiquity they were extraordinarily common, thanks to this conception, which promoted old superstition by lending an appearance of justification to the usage. Amulets also were provided with supernatural potency through certain ceremonies which are described in the magical papyri; engraved stones, of which vast numbers are to be found in our museums, were furnished with magical inscriptions and representations of gods or daimones to increase their potency. To go into the concept of power in magic would merely burden our description needlessly and be of no use, for the idea of potency, more or less clearly expressed, always underlies magic.

This concept of power is a fundamental factor in the idea which late antiquity held of the world and nature, and also in the religious innovations, and forms the most marked difference between the earlier and the later religion of Greece. In the higher religion, it explained the gods' interventions in the course of world events and the destiny of mankind; the concentration of interest in the gods' power thrust their personality into the background and thus forwarded the tendency to monotheism. In mysticism, God and the soul were resolved into potencies. In the lower religion, belief in power spread wider still. With its 'physical' explanations it legitimized belief in daimones, marvels, magic, sorcery, divination, and amulets, and contributed much to the continual spread of every sort of superstition, belief in sorcery, and other aberrations which marked the last age of antiquity. Looked at from this side, it was a relapse into savagery, and it is the irony of fate that science helped to bring about this result.

The Christians shared the general ideas of the time, including those concerning power, but Christianity ennobled them by lifting them to the religious plane. The word *phos*, light or illumination, signifies frequently in Christian writings a related idea, whereas in those of the pagans only the beginning of such a use appears, although light plays an uncommonly large part in pagan theology and magic. The word *charis*, grace, which is associated with the circle of ideas above described, has shed its connexion with natural forces and designates powers out of the ordinary as the gift of God's grace.

The late antique cosmology and the contemporary idea of power are very closely connected with each other. The picture of the world was held together by the doctrine of power, as its modern equivalent is held together by that of gravitation and, we may perhaps add, of chemical affinities which to a certain extent have a kind of correspondence to the doctrine which late antiquity held concerning sympathy and antipathy; but the great and essential difference is this, that while our picture of the universe belongs entirely to natural science, is mechanical and its forces precisely measured and reckoned, late antiquity's picture had from the very beginning its attachments in religion. Its first principle, called by Aristotle the unmoved mover, was at the same time the supreme God, conceived by less philosophic minds as the supreme Ruler of the universe. As it is said in a passage quoted later in this book from the work *On the Universe*, God guides the world with the powers which emanate from Him. So also did the stars guide the destiny of the world by means of the powers emanating from them. As conceived by late antiquity, power was mysterious, occult, and mystical. This

opened the way for occultism and mysticism, also for the
highest form of mysticism, *unio mystica*, which Hermetism
put in this way, that the power inherent in the human soul
unites with and passes into the highest Power, God.

4. ASTROLOGY

Astrology occupies so important a place in researches into
the religion of late antiquity that one can hardly open a book
or read an article on the subject without coming across it.
Also we find, as a self-evident proposition, expressed or understood, that every idea or symbol which has anything to do
with astrology is *ipso facto* shown to be of Eastern origin.
The foundation of astrology is Babylonian, the belief in the
influence of the stars on life on earth and the fate of man,
and the characterizing of the separate influence of every star
in accordance with the character of the god whose name it
bears; but so far as we know Babylonian astrology, it put the
phenomena in the vault of heaven on the same level as other
signs and omens.

The fundamental works on ancient astrology, which were
produced in Egypt in the second century B.C. and go under
the names of Nechepso-Petosiris and Hermes Trismegistos,
display on the other hand a thoroughly worked-out system;
we may venture to call it scientific after its fashion, which
depends upon the cosmology already dealt with. That the
system of astrology was worked out on the basis of the results
of Greek science is proved by the fact that it follows the
Hellenistic order of the planets as given above, whereas the
Babylonians down to the end of their civilization had a
different and arbitrary order, Moon, Sun—which usually are
not included in the series—Jupiter, Venus, Mercury, Saturn,
Mars. The system is constructed on strictly mathematical
lines, one might say trigonometrical, for the strength of the
influence of the heavenly bodies is reckoned like a parallelo-
gram of force, according to their reciprocal relations one to
another and their position in the Zodiac. To calculate a

nativity, that is to say the position of the stars at the moment
of a birth, which determined the child's life and destiny, was
a complicated and technical operation, at once mathematical
and astronomical, for which considerable specialist knowledge
was needed. Astrologers are often called mathematicians,
mathematici, also.

Astrology applied the law of causality strictly and without
exceptions. The universe was a kind of gigantic piece of
clockwork, whose wheels were geared into each other. If one
knew the movement of one wheel, that of the rest could be
calculated; since the motions of the stars could be calculated,
the events of an earthly life could be foretold from them.
Regarded from that angle, astrology was a scientific hypothesis on a grand scale, which believed it had the means of
solving the equation of the universe which Dubois Reymond
once made so famous. That is the explanation of its power,
for thousands of years, even over the clearest and keenest-
thinking intelligences, down to Tycho Brahe and Kepler. The
strict causality which astrology applied excluded any arbitrary
interference; everything that happens is conditioned by a
cause and governed by law, and the gods have no more
power than men to do anything against it. Since all divine
intervention is excluded, astrology led logically to atheism.
This conclusion was reached by some few, for instance the
Emperor Tiberius, but most people failed to understand
the complete and necessary consequences of astrological
determinism, which came into conflict with another conception, as self-evident to man as that of causality, namely
freewill.

This side of astrology was over the heads of ordinary folk.
They thought of astrologers as interpreters of omens, diviners
who were abler than the rest; for them, the planetary powers
were gods whom, maybe, one could appease like others with
sacrifices and prayers or master through magical means. After
all, the planets were named after gods and the constellations
had names out of mythology. Astrology became popular,

and as soon as that happens to any science, the demand arises
to make it accessible to the man in the street, in fact to
popularize it. This movement got under way as a result of
the introduction of the Julian calendar, which followed the
course of the sun, in the decades immediately preceding the
birth of Christ. The older oriental calendars, save that of
Egypt, had the cyclic lunar year, varying between twelve and
thirteen months, whose position relative to the solar year
changed nearly as much as that of Easter. With such a
calendar it was a very complicated task to calculate the
celestial phenomena; but when Caesar, in 46 B.C., introduced
the calendar which we still use with the correction added by
Pope Gregory XIII in 1582, and which agrees better with
the solar year, and the Emperor Augustus encouraged the
introduction in the East of calendars on the same basis, the
general public had in its hands a convenient means of making
the simpler astrological calculations. The Zodiac, in which
lie the orbits of the heavenly bodies, was easy to find, and
the sun entered a new sign on the 25th of each month. The
system was simplified to the doctrine which Trimalchio accepted and which we find in farmers' almanacs and occasionally
even in modern writings, that the character and destiny of a
man are determined by the sign of the zodiac under which
he is born.

The movement of the planets could not be read off from
the calendar, but a convenient way was found of taking them
also into account by connecting them with the seven days of
the week, which became popular at the same time. Although
the order of the days of the week is different, yet it too rests
on the Hellenistic order of the planets, Saturn, Jupiter, Mars,
the Sun, Venus, Mercury, the Moon. Behind it lies the
preconception that the planets, in regular order, govern each
an hour of the twenty-four which make up the day; the
calculation begins with Saturn. If Saturn governs the first
hour of a day (which is the meaning of the name Saturday),
$3 \times 7 = 21$, and the twenty-fifth hour, the first of the next

day, is governed by the Sun. Continuing the calculation in the same way, we come out to our order of the days of the week, Moon, Mars, Mercury, Jupiter, Venus. The Greeks translated the names of the Babylonian planetary gods by Greek ones, the Romans by Latin ones, and the Germans, who adopted the planetary week while they were still heathens, replaced the Latin names by those of native gods.

Although this detailed account of astrology may seem to fall outside the bounds of religious ideas, it has been necessary to clear matters up and give a better understanding of its effect on religious conceptions, both positively and negatively. No religious movement and no mysteries could escape the influence of astrology, but embodied more or less of it in their doctrine; here we must distinguish between the specifically astrological view of the world and the older and more general picture which lay behind it. We have already mentioned the ascent of the soul to heaven through the seven spheres of the planets; it is observable in Mithraism, Hermetism, and Gnosticism, in which certain sects supposed that each sphere was guarded by a 'toll-collector' who prevented the soul getting any farther if it did not know the right password. Among the mystery-religions, that of Mithra especially took in much from astrology, but the others were not unaffected by it either; Attis is called the 'shepherd of the bright stars'. We hear much of a god called Aion, a curious figure shown under weird shapes, who can almost be interpreted as the continuance of the universe; this is also symbolized by the image of a snake with its tail in its mouth, an allusion to the astrological doctrine of the cyclic destruction and renewal of the world, when all the planets come together in the sign of Cancer or Capricorn.

The astrological view of the universe could arouse a mystical feeling in the presence of such a picture of the world. Modern man shudders as he faces the infinitude of the universe of stars and is dizzied when he looks out on the whirling universe; he is caught by the mysticism of infinity. The admiration of the

ancients was directed to the order and obedience to law of the
universe, to which they attached an ethical, indeed a mystical, value. We speak of astral mysticism; according to what
Cicero says in the *Dream of Scipio*, the blessedness of the
elect soul consists in contemplating, from the highest heaven,
the eternal and regular movements of the celestial bodies.
The one poet of the earlier Empire who shows anything
which could be called religious enthusiasm is the author of an
astrological poem, Manilius, who professes his faith in the
astrological necessity, *heimarméne*, in an often-quoted line,

Fate rules the world, and laws that none escape.

The Stoics were not far from a similar conception, seeing
that their fundamental principle was the intelligence immanent in the universe and they emphasized the wise regulation
of the world according to plan. They admired, with an
almost religious reverence, its living and working in everything else and the risings and settings of the heavenly powers.
This feeling rose to self-abnegation; they put their fate in
the hands of divine providence, in other words, handed themselves over to *heimarméne*. The Stoics were able to allow a
breath of personality to their first principle; man realized
his insignificance and bowed before the divine omnipotence
and omniscience, but there was no room for childlike trust
in a Father. Still less could the astrologer reach it. His self-
abnegation in face of the causal nexus of destiny goes against
the innermost nature of man and must end in dull resignation or else in an attempt to escape from the senselessness
of fate.

Astrological determinism is a product of the inexorably
logical Greek thought, which could not have come about if
it had not been Greeks who constructed the astrological
system. Thus arose the problem of the relation of the gods
to fate, which is lacking in the oriental religions because in
them fate was simply the will of the gods. Religion is man's
protest against the meaninglessness of events, which is con-

tained in mechanical causality. With this no religion can compromise, for it does away with divine powers and human free will. From the time of Poseidonios on, philosophy found a way out, by supposing that the bodily existence of man was subject to destiny, but not his soul; Hermetism and Gnosticism had the same doctrine, and Christian baptism freed man from *heimarméne*, as did initiation into the mysteries. In the *Metamorphoses* of Apuleius it is blind, merciless fate which is the cause of Lucius' mishaps, until he is released from its power by initiation into the mysteries of Isis, for Isis is mistress of fate.

The pressure of blind, merciless, unavoidable destiny drove men into the arms of religion, which offered them a refuge from its insensate rule. They took their revenge by making the planetary gods into evil powers. For the Babylonians, the stars were tyrants and arbitrary, but they were not exclusively bad, for they could send not only evil but also good, namely, good luck. The mystical forms of religion in late antiquity made them into evil powers, which clad the soul, when sent down from heaven to earth to be incarnated into a human body, with its vices. This condemnation of the planetary powers arose as a protest against the doctrine of fate as mechanical causality which fettered man in bonds of iron and hung over him like an intolerable burden, since it excluded every kind of freedom, stripped him of his free will, and shut off his hopes of the grace of the gods. Under the crippling belief in fate, the truly religious took refuge in the haven of religious mysticism.

5. MONOTHEISM

With the help of dynamism and of the mathematics which reckoned the powers emanating from the stars, astrology let the machine of the universe run itself; there was no room for divine intervention. But this assumption of an all-controlling mechanical causality met with strong opposition. For anyone who would not recognize it, there remained the orderly plan of the universe, which could be explained only on the supposition that it came from a supreme regulating Intelligence. There was need of a supreme Ruler of the universe, a God. The train of thought which proves the existence of God from the purposeful arrangement of the universe, the teleological argument, is already represented by Xenophon as being put forward by Sokrates, and later it appears continually.

Monotheism had long been known to Greek philosophers. The founder of the Eleatic philosophy, Xenophanes, who flourished in the second half of the sixth century B.C., proclaimed that

> One God there is, greatest of gods and men,
> Unlike in form to mortals and in mind.

One of Sokrates' disciples, Antisthenes, said that there were indeed many gods according to human belief, but according to nature, only one. This conviction, which formerly had merely been held by certain philosophers, made its way farther and farther in the Hellenistic period. A contributory cause of this was the spread of philosophy to wider circles, even to the general public, owing to the preaching of wandering popular philosophers. It was not without a certain importance that the old belief in the gods was so weakened that people spoke less often than formerly of particular gods, but used general expressions, as 'the god' or 'the deity'. All this, however, was merely preparatory, and the triumph of monotheism had its origin in several circumstances; besides philosophy, which conceived of its first principle as the supreme God, there was the cosmology, which called for a supreme Ruler of the universe, the monarchical government of the State, which encouraged a monarchical régime not only on earth but in heaven, and finally syncretism and kathenotheism, which resolved other gods into the particular deity to whom the worshipper turned.

It is not necessary to go into philosophical monotheism, with its identification of the supreme principle with God, whether Aristotle's 'first origin' which sets all else in motion without being moved itself, or the transcendent Platonic or the immanent Stoic deity. It is sufficient to remind ourselves that this philosophic god, for those who indulged in profounder thinking about religion, was the self-evident final result of their theology, but by no means ruled out polytheism; philosophy made room also for the old gods in its system of doctrine.

The philosophical doctrine that there is but one God, one Power, called, after its various manifestations, by various names, became a generally held opinion under the Empire. The great popular orator Dion Chrysostom says:

Some tell us that Apollo, Helios and Dionysos are one and the same ... and generally reduce all the gods to a single force or power.

A century later Maximus of Tyre declares that,

amid all this strife and contention [sc., about other questions], you may see all the world over one generally accepted opinion and doctrine, that there is one God, King and Father of all, and also many gods who are God's children and share His sovranty. This is what the Greek says, and so also says the barbarian.

To this conviction the concept of power contributed, as is hinted in Dion's phraseology, in so far as it directed interest rather to the power of God than to His personality. The older expressions to theion, hoi theoi, were replaced by to kreitton, hoi kreittones, 'might', 'the mighty', 'mights'. This line of thought ended in the deism of late antiquity, represented for instance by the contemporary of the Emperor Julian, Ammianus Marcellinus, the last ancient historian of importance. He seldom speaks of the old gods, and if he does, he appeals to the concept of power, but he often uses such expressions as 'the celestial God', 'the heavenly', or 'the supreme Being'; it is significant that he rarely uses the Latin word deus but regularly numen, which has a less definite meaning and implies divine power. This pale deism was very convenient for pagan panegyrists who had to deliver speeches in praise of Christian Emperors.

From the new cosmology, which emphasized the orderliness of the universe, philosophy concluded that the world must be regulated by a supreme Ruler. Aristotle had already ended the twelfth book of the *Metaphysics* that that which exists must not be ill governed, and adds a quotation from Homer,

No multitude of lords; let one bear sway!

Among Aristotle's works a highly interesting book has wandered. It is a treatise *On the Universe* composed in the first century A.D.; there is a useful English version by E. S. Foster in vol. iii of the Oxford translation of Aristotle edited by J. A. Smith and W. D. Ross. Its unknown author, after giving a dry sketch of the universe and its arrangement, is seized in the concluding chapters by genuine religious enthusiasm when he speaks of the Supreme Ruler of the universe. His expressions are so enlightening for the power of the then cosmology to forward monotheism and for the contribution of dynamism thereto, that a short epitome is appropriate here.

Everything, he says, originates from God and through God, and is maintained by Him, but if for that reason anyone asserts that the world is full of gods, that is true enough of the divine powers but not of the essence of Deity, for God does not work toilsomely nor with His hands, but, being in possession of an unwearying power, He governs what is distant as well as what is near. God occupies the highest and most eminent place. The body, or sphere, which is nearest to Him (the planetary spheres) has the most experience and benefit of His power, then the parts next in order, and so on till we come to the earth, which is farthest removed from God's sustaining activity, wherefore all things upon it are weak, irregular, and full of confusion; nevertheless, God's

sustaining force reaches even it. It is proper and most fitting
to conceive that God's power and might, which has its place
in heaven, is the reason why all things are maintained, even
the most distant; but it is not proper to suppose that God
personally performs that which occurs upon earth. By a
simple movement of that which is foremost and nearest to
Him, God extends His power to that which is connected
with it and beyond that to what lies farther off, till it spreads
through the whole. This holds good also for the structure
of the universe. By a simple circular movement of the
celestial vault the various orbits of the heavenly bodies are
caused, some moving faster, others slower, all according to
their distances. For this reason the universe is called *kosmos*,
order. As in a chorus all the members keep in tune with what
their leader starts and thus a harmonious concert of voices
results, so God leads and guides the world; according to the
signal given by Him from on high, the stars and the sky move
and the seasons change. All that happens in the universe is
set in motion by a single impulse, invisible and beyond the
reach of our observation, and the individual phemonema are
the result. The soul is invisible, but can be detected by its
activity, human culture; God, Who is the mightiest in power
and the most glorious in beauty, Who possesses everlasting
life and perfection of all that is good, can similarly be
detected in His work. God is conceived as living in heaven;
the most excellent of visible things, the heavenly bodies, are
there also, and they alone are everlastingly in the same order
and are never altered, nor change their course as things on
earth do, for these are easily changed and exposed to many
vicissitudes. What the helmsman is to a ship, the choir-
leader to the dances of a chorus, the laws to a State, the
general to an army, that God is to the world, with this
exception, that He does not grow weary but is free from
toil and from bodily weakness. Enthroned at an immovable
point, he sets all in motion and makes it circle where and
how He will, in various forms and fashions of life.

Although God is one, our author continues, He has many names, for He is titled according to the activities which He himself originates. We call Him Zes or Zeus, that is to say, lifegiver and accomplisher, son of Kronos, that is, Chronos, Time, because He endures from one endless age to another, lightener and thunderer, Lord of light and of the ether, sender of thunderbolts and rain, giver of increase, protector of cities, guardian, God of kinship and inheritance, protector of friendship, amity, and hospitality, Lord of hosts, giver of victory, God of purification and atonement, merciful, gracious, saviour, true deliverer, in short Lord of heaven and earth, having a title from everything that occurs or happens in Nature, because He alone is the origin of all. By Necessity (*ananke*) or Fate is meant Zeus. 'All' means nothing else than 'God', as Plato says: 'God, as an ancient saying has it, holding the beginning, the middle and the end of everything, goes on a straight path, moving in accordance with His nature; and Justice follows Him to punish transgressions of the divine law, and he who shall be blessed holds fast by her.'

All this exposition, detailed as it is and full of genuine feeling, depends upon the new cosmology and upon the idea of power, which serves not only to explain God's activity in the world but also to exalt Him as far as possible above it, without however separating Him from it. The last section calls the supreme God Zeus, as was the Stoic custom, and supports that with a list of Zeus' epithets and functions— a tribute to the old religion which remained ineffective, for Zeus was too laden with mythology and local worships to put on the mantle of the Supreme Being, as that age wanted Him. The author of the treatise *Concerning the Universe* took over ideas from sundry schools of philosophy and worked them into a popular theology, which in his day not only answered to the needs of the educated but undoubtedly penetrated quite far down.

We may venture on this statement because of the popu-

larity of astrology in that age. It was founded on the new
cosmology and emphasized the rule of law in the ordering
of the universe. In its scientific form, indeed, as mechanical
causality, it excluded God, but in His place came the belief
of the common people in astral deities. This developed a
theology, in the older (Oriental) form of which the sky-god
Caelus was at the head of the universe, but under Greek
influence, the chief intermediary being Stoic philosophy,
the sun-god took his place; we have already learned of his
position as coryphaeus of the planets.

Solar religion to some extent answered to what appears
to be the natural result of the development of Greek religion
on its own principles, a general cosmological religion for the
whole world. The Emperors encouraged it, for in it they
found an expression for their own majesty; as the sun-god
ruled the universe, so his earthly copy, the Emperor, ruled
the world. Aurelian introduced sun-cult as the State
religion, and we still have a reminder of this in the date
of Christmas, the rebirth of the unconquerable Sun at the
winter solstice. It is beyond doubt that the monarchical
government of the State, which had been the prevailing
form since the Hellenistic period began, and particularly
since the Roman Empire became a really world-wide domina-
tion, contributed largely to promote monotheism. For the
world of the gods is everywhere, in pagan religion, modelled
after the constitution of the State. There must be but one
ruler on heaven, as on earth. To understand adequately the
effect of this thought in the earlier Imperial times, the
student should read Dion Chrysostom's orations on kingship,
which throughout draw a parallel between God's government and that of a good Emperor. The monarchical and
well-organized form of the State under the Emperors made
the idea appear natural that the universe was controlled by
a supreme Governor enthroned in the heavens.

Nevertheless, sun-cult did not win the day; it remained the
religion rather of the State than the people. The sun-god

was handicapped by his physical and phenomenal form, and sun-cult was too cosmological, in its way too scientific, to give the people the god they wanted, a god in whom the worshipper could have confidence and from whom he might find comfort and help. But solar symbolism was so influential that it is often found in Christian writings; Christ appears as the Sun of Righteousness, and beside Him the Church is symbolized by the moon.

It was a weakness for pagan monotheism in its fight against Judaism and Christianity, which was gaining many adherents simply because of its strict monotheism, that it never cleared the old polytheism away; the old gods survived as subordinate deities, satraps of the supreme God. We have already seen that they were likewise interpreted as manifestations of the supreme God in various departments, and that the omnipotence of Zeus was proved by listing his numerous functions and epithets. Something of the kind is to be found in a poem ascribed to Orpheus, which comes near to being grotesque in its eagerness to include everything in the universe in the body of Zeus. A goddess who in vigorous language laid claim to the same omnipotence was Isis, but she, like Zeus, remained after all merely one of the old deities. A phenomenon which is known in the history of religion as kathenotheism occurs when the worshipper, turning wholeheartedly to some one deity, makes him overshadow the rest, so that he stands forth as the only one; this is often to be found in hymns to, and prose eulogies of, a particular god. Some gods receive the epithet *pantheos*, 'all-god', and we even find a god named Pantheos. This too can be called a preliminary to monotheism.

With this was connected the old idea that, although deities may have different names among different peoples, it is still the same gods who are worshipped under these names, as the sun and moon are the same the world over although their names differ, to quote Plutarch. It was this doctrine which Celsus put forward in his controversial treatise

against Christianity. His *True Doctrine* was a harmony of
the pagan traditions concerning God and the gods, conceived in the same way as in the theological system which
the Neoplatonists constructed towards the close of antiquity
in conscious opposition to Christianity, the last word of
pagan theology.

This syncretistic doctrine adopted, towards the close of
antiquity, oracles, which again came forward as guides in
matters of religion. There exists a considerable number of
monotheistic oracles, which were collected at the beginning
of the Middle Ages by way of proof that even the heathen
had some notion of the true doctrine; some of these oracles
are genuine, others are counterfeit. The oracle whose activities are best known is that of Apollo of Klaros near
Kolophon in Asia Minor. To it is ascribed a declaration
that Iao is the highest god of all, that he is Hades in winter,
Zeus in spring, Helios in summer, and Dionysos in autumn.
This oracle is not so extraordinary as it sounds. The Jewish
God was widely known in Asia Minor, where he was identified sometimes with Zeus, sometimes with Dionysos, and
the idea that the god sleeps in the winter and rises when spring
begins was native to those parts. No doubt prevails that
Jewish monotheism exercised a strong influence and a
decided attraction for the pagans. An often-quoted poem,
which was fathered on Orpheus to make it more effective,
proclaims the omnipotence of the one God in language which
to some extent is borrowed from the Old Testament.

If from the famous and much-disputed speech before the
Areiopagos at Athens which the Acts of the Apostles put
into the mouth of St. Paul we subtract the references to the
Jewish God and to the eschatology which is so prominent a
point in Pauline religion, the discourse in which St. Paul sets
forth his message is one which an educated pagan might well
have pronounced.

God that made the world and all things therein, seeing that he
is Lord of heaven and earth, dwelleth not in temples made with

hands, neither is worshipped with men's hands, as though he needed any thing, seeing that he giveth to all life, and breath, and all things... though he be not far from every one of us, for in him we live, and move, and have our being; as certain also of your own poets have said, For we also are his offspring. Forasmuch then as we are the offspring of God, we ought not to think that the Godhead is like unto gold, or silver, or stone, graven by art and man's device.

Pagan monotheism was no more than a tendency, although it was an important and all-embracing religious thought; it did not uproot polytheism either in cult or in theology, but let its many gods be subordinated to or absorbed in the Supreme Deity. The result was that it imprinted, not only on the minds of the educated but on those of the vulgar, the conviction that one God is at the helm of the universe. On this inheritance the jealous Christian God, Who tolerated no other gods besides Himself, entered. By the elimination of the subordinate deities, the supreme God showed mightier than ever in lonely majesty. Pagan monotheism did much preparatory work for Christianity, and the Christians knew it and appealed to it.

6. TRANSCENDENTALISM

The philosophy which treats of the realities lying beyond the data of the senses was founded by Plato, who looked behind the changeful and perishable world of things to the eternal and imperishable world of Forms; but Plato held firmly to the old religion and did not consider himself a religious reformer but a philosopher, a seeker after truth, a scientist; and so he was considered by his own contemporaries and the age next following. After the intervening centuries had indeed given it impulses from many quarters but not put it in the foreground of men's interest, transcendentalism was taken up by Plotinos, the founder of Neoplatonism, who flourished in the middle of the third century A.D., as his central idea, and was extended, building on the foundations Plato had laid, to a profoundly thoughtful and wide-reaching philosophic system having a deeply religious content. Thus, by the disclosure of the religious content of Plato's thinking, he became, half a millennium after his death, one of the world's greatest religious leaders, giving utterance in thought and word to one of the deepest and most abundant sources of religion.

Religious transcendentalism has other than a philosophic origin. It arises from the mystic sensation of union with the highest, the divine, the overwhelming, in that moment of rapture when the human soul finds itself set free from the fetters of the body and exalted above the sensuous; a religious experience which is common to the mystics of all times and all countries. The result is a marked dualism, a contempt for the corporeal, which, as being a hindrance to union with the divine, appears not only perishable but actually evil, and a prizing of the supersensuous as eternal and precious. It is the same opposition which in Plato obtains between the changing, perishable world of phenomena and the eternal and imperishable one of the Forms.

We can follow the growth of religious transcendentalism in the little treatises, important from the religious point of view, which are collected under the name of Hermes Trismegistos; they are of different centuries, the oldest being probably of the first Christian century. The great debt they owe to Greek philosophy is obvious, although an attempt has been made to undervalue it in favour of influence from the East, which appears most clearly in prophetic and missionary zeal and enthusiasm. More evident is Jewish influence, which has given rise to a not altogether false conjecture that the Hermetic writings are the work of hellenizing Jews in Egypt, in which country influences from all quarters crossed each other and coalesced.

An older group of these writings is full of a pantheistic, universal mysticism, originating in Stoicism, and an optimistic view of the universe which is connected with it. God is the creator and lord of all, as man may see in His work;

the universe is a second God, an immortal being; God is the One, and everything is full of God; He is the invisible, the Most High, Who is seen in the mind (*nous*). Everything is in Him, everything comes from Him, He gives all and takes nothing; He is all that becomes, all that does not become, the thought which is thought, the creating Father, the active God, the good which makes all things. The Stoic arsenal may have provided the idea, but it is vivified by a new spirit which is more impregnated with mysticism than in Poseidonios, more personal than in Epiktetos. The same tendency is to be found in the way the world is regarded. It is the image of God, a material God, while man is the image of the world. At the same time, the world is said to be beautiful, but not good; the problem of evil will not let itself be forgotten.

The spirit of man resembles God in its unbounded power of raising itself above the world to heaven and including everything in itself; but if we confine the soul to the body, we cannot learn to know anything, and lack of knowledge of the divine is the highest evil. This omnipresence of the soul is not the flight of the mind which soars over and examines heaven and earth, but the mystic feeling of unity with the All which is to be won by contemplation. The religious transcendentalism which breaks out in this feeling bursts the bounds of Stoicism, for it endeavours to exalt God as much as possible and seeks to approach the highest not by the work of the intellect but by divine enlightenment.

At the roots of Hermetism lies, not the logical connexion of thoughts and ideas, but the mystical longing after a God sufficiently exalted to satisfy man's striving after the highest, the overwhelming, to find his rest and peace in the divine. The mystic desires at once the exalted distance of God and union with or absorption into Him. This religious feeling clothed itself in such forms as were available, first in Stoicism, which made room for mysticism with Poseidonios. His God, being immanent in everything, satisfied to some extent the

mystical feeling of unity with the All and the mystic's longing for unity with the divine; but the mystic demanded not
only unity with God but also that He should be exalted,
for if that were not so, union with God lost its value, since
that consists in the beatific consciousness of the disappearance
of the intervening distance and of union with or absorption
into Deity. Therefore the Stoic doctrine of the immanence
of God and His omnipresence served as a preliminary, but
the experience which is at the foundation of Hermetic
mysticism led to an emphasizing of God's exaltedness and
necessarily ended in transcendentalism, which alone could
satisfy the longings of the mystic and fully answer to his
experience of God.

This development, prescribed as it was by the inner nature
of mysticism, led to the shape which transcendentalism
assumes in the later treatises, the group which is dualistic
and pessimistic in character. God, they teach, is free from
becoming and from movement, only He is the good. God
is high above the world, thinkable only for us, not for Himself; He is neither intelligence, spirit nor light, but the cause
of them. Since God is exalted above being, the problem
arose how the world came into being, since its connexion
with God was excluded by transcendentalism. In one
tractate the will of God appears as the intermediary; the
work is God's will and it is His nature to will everything;
He wills all but does not do it, says the author. Another
intermediary is Logos, conventionally rendered 'word'.

The most discussed of the Hermetic writings, the first,
which has the title *Poimandres*, begins with a cosmogony, as
already stated. *Logos* is here the word of power, 'God said,
Let there be light, and there was light', and Logos precisely
in that capacity is suitable as the intermediary between the
transcendent God and the created world, and is so introduced
in that treatise. But it looks as if the author had had his
doubts because of the rationalistic connotation, the tendency
towards signifying the activity of the intellect, which the

word *logos* has in Greek, and so he puts by the side of Logos
the Nous-Demiourgos, Intelligence the Creator, who is said
to be of like nature with Logos. Man was created by the
Father of the whole as a brother to Logos and to Nous-
Demiourgos. He united in love with Nature, and thence was
born in the fullness of time mankind and the world. Anthro-
pos, primal Man, who plays a great and much-discussed role
in many mystical teachings and is conceived of as an intermediary, takes no such part here; his origin is meant to
explain the twofold nature of man, mortal as regards his
body, immortal as sharing in true humanity. This account
has been rightly called a myth of original sin.

The creation-myth in the *Poimandres* is confused, put
together from mutually contradictory elements, partly mystical, partly belonging to natural philosophy, and does not
wholly exclude mythology from God, but the attempt to
exalt Him above all matter is decidedly to the fore, while in
the concluding hymn He is called 'unutterable' and invoked
by means of silence, that is to say, the silent mystical contemplation, which ends in the rapture of voiceless ecstasy.
This is described and emphasized time and again in the
Hermetic writings as the source of true enlightenment
(*gnosis*). It illumines the intelligence and soul of man,
exalts it, and transforms it into the nature of God. The
soul, even while housed in a mortal body, can be deified if
it contemplates the beauty of the Good. Hermes says to his
son Tat, 'I am gone out of myself into an immortal body
and am no longer what I was, but am born in mind (*nous*).'

For the Hermetics, as for all mystics, the corporeal is the
evil, because it hinders ecstatic union with God. The good
is identified with God, as in Plotinos; the good and God cannot be separated, nothing is good but God alone. What is
created is full of sufferings, or passions; now what is suffering cannot be the good, and becoming is a 'suffering' in itself. The good cannot be in what becomes, that is, in the
world, but only in the not-becoming, with God. With man,

the good is but the least portion of evil. The world is the fullness of evil, God the fullness (*pléroma*) of good.

Since the world is evil and the body is evil, the problem presents itself how man can be freed from evil. The Hermetic solution is simple: 'the man who has enlightenment (*gnosis*) must recognize himself', meaning that divine enlightenment, ecstatic union with God, brings salvation. If man knows that he is formed from life and light, he will turn towards life. He who recognizes himself passes into the overflowing stream of good; he who loves the body, which is the result of an amorous fault (original sin), will remain wandering about in darkness and suffering, enduring through the senses that which belongs to death.

There is a surprising dictum that it is due to man's ignorance that he calls the gods and some human beings good, whereas only God is good and none of the other so-called gods, or human beings, is or can be good. However, this statement is not so remarkable if it is put into its proper relation with the cosmology which the Hermetics, like others, accepted in the form developed by astrology. We have already met its teaching concerning the passage of the soul up and down through the planetary spheres, by which it is clothed by the planets with its human qualities and defects, and Hermetism speaks of the movements of the stars and other heavenly bodies. It was vital for it to come to an understanding with the astrological conception of fate, the inescapable chain of cause and effect known as *heimarméne*, because no serious religion, least of all a mystical one, can hold that the supreme God is subject to fate, nor identify Him with it. As Hermetism was quite clear about its transcendental conception of God, it was obliged to deny the power of fate over the soul and confine it to the body; the man who possesses enlightenment is immortal and has power over everything, but although he is exalted above the planets, yet his body is their slave. The planetary forces and *heimarméne* are evil powers, which rule the corporeal world, consequently the perceptible gods, the planets, are evil gods. Only the transcendental God, who is superior to the world of sense, is good. The Hermetics, like everyone else, accepted the new cosmology in its astrological shape, but they provided it with a transcendental superstructure; they did not, as had previously been done, draw the line of demarcation between the sublunary and superlunary worlds but between the sensuous and the supersensuous.

Gnosticism drew the same line of demarcation. This was the Christian offshoot of the stock of ideas which is known as *gnosis* and finds its pagan expression in Hermetism. Gnosticism flourished in the second and third centuries A.D. and involved Christianity in a serious danger of being drawn into the ferment of metaphysical speculations; but the Church was so fortunate as to overcome it, though not without difficulty, thanks to her stable organization, while Gnosticism was split into numerous sects and every Gnostic teacher spoke with his own tongue according to the promptings of his higher enlightenment. Here only those traits can be brought to notice which were current among the majority of Gnostics and are of interest in this connexion.

The Gnostics' God is incomprehensible, inexpressible, transcendent, and the transcendent superstructure of the universe is full of the Aeons which emanate from Him, often appearing in pairs. The problem for such a dualistic view was, as always, to contrive a connexion between the transcendent and the sensuous worlds, and this was done by making one of the Aeons, often the lowest, descend to the world of sense, where it is broken up and imprisoned. Even in man there is a spark of the supersensuous, or he has a prototype in the supersensuous world. His deliverance is brought about by God, or one of the Aeons, sending a supersensuous being down to earth to liberate this supersensuous spark which is in man from the bonds of the sensuous and bring it back to its celestial origin. This is the point at which Gnosticism could connect with Christianity, for this deliverer

was made out to be Christ, more or less transformed by
metaphysics. Gnosticism adopted astrology and, as time
went on, increasing mythological elements, until one of its
later writings is largely taken up with the passwords which
the soul must pronounce during its ascent to heaven in order
to pass the guardians of the planetary spheres and make its
way up to the highest heaven.

Gnosticism was an attempt to restate Christianity and
express it in terms and ways of thought which fitted the
natural science and philosophy of the time. The outstanding
problem of transcendentalism was the relation between the
transcendent and the sensuous worlds. From the religious
point of view that divides into two problems. One was
cosmological, the creation of the world; the other and more
serious was anthropological, the doctrine of salvation, or the
question how the soul is to be set free from the material
universe and return to its home in the transcendental world.
The resemblance between Gnosticism and Hermetism in
their fundamental conceptions is obvious; both accepted
the new cosmology and provided it with a transcendental
superstructure, but whereas Hermetism did not describe the
transcendental world in any detail, Gnosticism introduced
a speculative system of Aeons or heavens in many gradations.
The fundamental idea of their doctrine of original sin is the
same; a being belonging to the higher world descended to
the lower; the great difference is in the doctrine of salvation.
In Hermetism this is attained by union with the Supreme
Being in the silent ecstasy experienced by the mystic, the
necessary conditions for which are holy stillness and the overcoming of the sense-perceptions. Hermetism has not yet
quite abandoned the standpoint of Greek philosophy, which
is that man is to gain his deliverance by his own power, but
it is on the way to seeking help from God. In one tractate
the disciple is advised to pray to the Lord and Father, the
Only, the One whence the One comes, for grace to conceive
of such a God. This does not tell us very much; the treatise

concerning rebirth is more lucid. Here Hermes says that
through the mercy of God he has passed into an immortal
body, quitting his own; that the true good is sown by the
will of God, and that he who attains regeneration is the son
of God, a man by the will of God. In Gnosticism the
doctrine of salvation develops into a drama which can be
called a myth of salvation, an account of how a part of the
supersensuous world got into the custody of matter and how
it is set free, after toil and struggle, by the emissary of the
higher world.

Ancient writers, both pagan and Christian, say that
Gnosticism has its origin in the wisdom of Greece, in philosophic mystic and astrological teaching; we must add
Christian doctrine also. This opinion, which is now almost
suppressed by a one-sided emphasis laid on Oriental influence,
contains a great deal of truth and is strengthened by the fact
that the great philosopher Plotinos found reason for refuting
Gnosticism at length. It represents the climax of syncretism,
which tried to weld together pagan and Christian speculation by importing into the latter certain ideas current in
the former.

The religious transcendentalism which is here described
is older than the break-through of transcendental ideas in
philosophy into the profoundly thought out system set up
by Plotinos in the middle of the third century A.D. Plotinos
had forerunners, among others the Platonizing Neopytha-
gorean Numenios of Apamea, who showed a strong predilection for Oriental wisdom and whose teaching so much
resembled that of Plotinos that the latter was said by ancient
critics to depend entirely upon him. Plotinos was an
Egyptian, like his revered teacher Ammonios Sakkas, one
of the men who left nothing behind in writing but whose
influence was immense, as is seen in his numerous disciples.
Both were profoundly religious men and it may reasonably
be asked if they did not receive impulses from the religious
thought of their age, which they purified, ennobled, and

refashioned into a construction of philosophic thought. This is not the place to describe Plotinos' philosophy, but only its religious side. God is exalted so far above all reality that only negative predications can be made of Him; He is not good, but the Good; this positive definition, inherited from Plato, led to a tension which Plotinos never quite overcame. His view of God's activity has been described as a doctrine of emanation, but also as dynamic pantheism. The life of the soul in the body is a disturbance of its original condition in the supersensuous world, and its separation from the body is its return to the higher existence which corresponds to its nature. Plotinos met with the difficulty, never overcome, of combining dualism with a monistic first principle.

The religious basis of Plotinos' philosophy appears clearly in his account of the means by which man can approach the First Principle, the One, God. That cannot be done by knowing or thinking, but only through experience of His presence, which is better than knowledge, by immediate contemplation and by the will to free oneself from all that binds man to earthly things. The soul, in its inmost nature, is capable of coming into contact with the One, for it is akin thereto, but is hindered by its connexion with what is corporeal. It must let go all positive determinations and capacities and approach its goal by the deepest concentration upon itself, by turning in upon itself and rejecting all consciousness, even self-consciousness. When, in the depths of the soul, the meeting with the divine is accomplished, the difference between the contemplator and the contemplated vanishes. God can only be observed or experienced, not described; it is an illumination which gives certainty that God exists, not knowledge of what He is. By this meeting man becomes divine and reveals his own proper divine nature. The soul perceives the source of life, the well-spring of thought, the beginning of existence, the origin of the good, the birth of the soul itself. This is mystical religion of the same kind as we found in Hermetism.

Neoplatonism was the ruling philosophy at and after the end of antiquity, but it did not remain on the philosophic heights where Plotinos had put it, but took up and interpreted more and more of the cults and religious practices of the time, incorporating more and more belief in daimones and magic with its system, while at the same time developing it scholastically. Plotinos' successor, Porphyry, already went very far in this direction and the man who gave Neoplatonism a decisive turn that way was Iamblichos, whom his disciples called 'the divine'. A treatise *On the Mysteries*, which is the most important and illuminating source of our knowledge of later Neoplatonic religious feeling, is his work.

All this composition is a defence of theurgy, the art of producing apparitions of gods and daimones, at the same time of magic, which posed as religion, and of divination, so far as that is theurgical; in this last respect it is akin to the magical texts and recipes which are preserved on Egyptian papyri. Theurgy brings about union with God, says this author, frees us from the mutability of the existence, exalts us to the eternal, bestows truth upon us, and breaks the bonds of fate. All this belongs to the occultism which will be treated in our next section. As an example of the scholastic we may cite the last great Neoplatonist, Proklos. Everything is brought into connexion through the origin of plurality from unity and its return to unity, and everything is divided into triads after the law of triadic development, namely, continuance in the origin, production from it, and return to it. In accordance with this there are inserted between the intelligible and the intellectual gods the gods who are at once intelligible and intellectual; their distinguishing quality is possession of powers. The intellectual, that is to say, the old gods, allegorically interpreted, are divided into sevens. We need go no farther, for these speculations have no religious interest.

Although the Neoplatonists were not concerned with the reality of the universe, the new cosmology was the founda-

tion of their theology. The concept of power had long
served to explain divination; it also explained the activity
of the gods and daimones in general. The gradations of the
picture of the universe had a corresponding feature in the
many classes into which souls, daimones, and gods were
divided, up to the highest, transcendent God. In this
cosmology, shaped with the help of the concept of power,
there was no difficulty in finding a place for the phenomena
which always occur in mystical and exalted movements, the
phenomena commonly called psychical, which are to be discussed in the next section. Even the ascent to the Supreme
Being in contemplative ecstasy is foreshadowed in a cosmology provided with a transcendental superstructure and
understood in a religious reinterpretation. The difference
between the perishable and faulty sublunar world and the
eternal and divine superlunary is enlarged into the difference
between the perishable, evil world of phenomena and that
which is divine and transcendental. Thus contempt for all
that is corporeal, and mysticism generally, found a place in
the cosmology which was originally based upon physical
science.

The form which the later Neoplatonists gave to paganism
is paganism's last word in the struggle with Christianity; it
is a theology whose profound religious and philosophical content cannot be denied, but it is disfigured by all manner of
magic and superstition, which is interpreted in a mystical
and allegorical spirit. How profoundly such doctrine could
grip one who was at the very summit of the culture of his
time is shown by the last champion of heathendom who sat
on the Imperial throne, Julian. His writings, full as they are
of firmly founded belief and warm religious feeling, are
wholly and entirely in the spirit of Iamblichos. He was a
devoted follower of the occultism to which Neoplatonism
had attached itself, by the help of which the mysteries were
reshaped and reinterpreted, and whose final basis was religious transcendentalism.

The God Whom the mystics beheld in the moment of ecstasy was accessible only to a minority who had the spiritual prerequisites for ecstatic contemplation, although He could be the object of religious speculation, as in Gnosticism. The idea of God entertained by transcendentalism, which makes the highest and true God be exalted above and separate from the world, was a philosophical and mystical principle which lacked vividness and form and could not satisfy a man who longed for a personal deity that should be close to him. If after all the transcendent God was a powerful ferment in the religious feeling of the time and produced much unrest, seeking, and controversy, the reason for that was that He had a resemblance and relationship—manifestly superficial yet inescapable—with the Supreme Ruler of the universe whom the new cosmology called for. It is only from that point of view that we can understand the effect of the transcendental conception of God in religious thought, pagan and Christian alike.

Man was a microcosmos, a model of the macrocosmos, and like it was divided into a material part, which was perishable, and a divine part, which was spiritual and imperishable. He longed for the higher world, freedom from the fetters of *heimarméne* or fate, and deliverance from the defects of the earth. In face of this vista the troubles of life, the misfortunes of society, and the despotism of the State all vanished. Portraits of Emperors and of holy men from the close of antiquity show the rapt look directed heavenwards which gazes into the higher world; it always shines from their eyes, the windows of the soul, with the same stereotyped expression. The body disappears, concealed by the drapery; the old delight in human beauty is gone. Thus art mirrors the revolution in the spiritual life and in the world of human ideas.

To end this section we may say a few words concerning the origin of the dualism which expressed itself in transcendentalism, because this is now generally looked for in

the doctrine of Zarathustra and a sufficient proof of the
orientalizing of Greek religion found therein. The dualism
which we found in Hermetism, Gnosticism, and Neoplatonism is the antithesis between the transcendent world
of the good and the evil, material world of phenomena; its
result is contempt for the world, attempts to escape from it,
asceticism, by which escape from the fetters of the body is
sought. Iranian dualism, on the other hand, accepts this
world and is active. The struggle between good and evil
goes on in this world, and it is the duty of the pious man to
advance the good by tilling the land, watching over his
house, bringing children into the world, and fighting evil by
exterminating noxious beasts and weeds. On the side of the
good god are light and day, all good men and beneficent
powers in Nature, useful animals and plants; on the side of
the evil god are darkness and night, wicked men, destructive
natural forces, harmful beasts, and poisonous plants. Iranian
dualism moves *in* this world, Greek dualism *between* this
world and the supersensuous one; this is a fundamental
distinction which cannot be glozed over in any way. The
origin of Greek dualism is not in the doctrine of Zarathustra
concerning the contest between good and evil in the world,
but in Plato's doctrine of the antithesis between the perishable and changeful world of phenomena and the eternal and
higher world of the Forms. This fountain-head is powerful
enough to teach us to understand the ability of the flood of
dualism to carry everything away with it. Iranian dualism
may have been interpreted in the Greek spirit and contributed to the spread of dualism, but it cannot be credited
with any great importance in the development of Greek
religious thought. But when we know the old connexions
between Greece and the Orient and know how lively they
became after the days of Alexander the Great; when we
hear that Greek was written in the chancellery of the
Arsakids, that Persian scribes produced business documents
in Greek at the same time, and that even Sapor I added a

Greek text to the newly discovered inscriptions recording his exploits; when we know the spread of art under Greek influence through to Eastern Asia, we do well to put the question, neglected and left unanswered by modern research, if Greek thought did not affect that of the East, especially in its dualistic ideas. When we realize the force of the Greek spirit, it would be very surprising if the stream of ideas moved only from east to west and not also from west to east.

7. OCCULTISM AND THEOSOPHY

The pure form in which transcendental religion appears in Plotinos and some of the Hermetic writings could be the property only of the elect, who thought deeply and had high endeavours. For a religious feeling of this kind to spread widely it must be popularized, building upon some spiritual disposition which is to be found in all times but whose development and spread depend on the temper of the age. This is to be found in some and is infectious. The practical side is occult practices and phenomena; religious experience of these is fundamental, whereas the doctrine, theosophy, always follows occultism as its theoretical shadow and takes on different forms according to the different intellectual views of the time.

Zealously pursued researches into the syncretism of late antiquity have concerned themselves mostly with doctrines and ideas; only in general terms and mostly in passing have they dealt with the soil from which these ideas and doctrines grew. And yet this is the most important and decisive point, for if these ideas and doctrines had not found a favourable and productive nursery, they would have withered away. Their origin is generally found in the East. Even during the centuries before the Persian War, Oriental influences poured out in a mighty flood over the Greeks, who took them up, but refined them and refashioned them in the Hellenic spirit. Why did the opposite occur in late antiquity? Why was the Greek world orientalized, especially in its religious aspect?

There is such a thing as conversion, not of the individual only but of humanity in general, and this took place in late antiquity; it was a conversion from rationalism to mystical and occultist belief. The problem is to find the reason for this conversion. There is no lack of means for attacking that problem; there is abundant material in many writings for the study of the religious experience (to use the phrase as William James does in his famous book) of late antiquity. The fundamental importance of the problem is so great that it deserves to be treated and illustrated.

Anyone who knows Latin literature from the beginning of the Empire is aware that despite prosperity a feeling of weariness spread over the ancient world. They were tired of seeking and researching and had put away science in favour of striving after a righteous and happy life. In our day, science has been represented as an enemy to religion, apt to destroy it. So it was in the later part of the classical age of Greece, but it is more correct to speak of rationalism than of science, for the sophists combated the belief in the gods with rationalistic arguments. The Greeks laid the foundations of science and made marvellous progress from Thales to Aristarchos of Samos, but Greek science had an inward weakness. It consisted chiefly in logical thinking, which, setting out from isolated, often insufficient observations, set up general laws. It has been made a reproach against it, and not without cause, that it lacked experiment, which is the vital nerve of modern science; at least it applied it on a quite inadequate scale. It is characteristic that the ancients went farthest in that science which depends upon observation only and excludes experiment, astronomy. Since experimental material was not increased, the mill of thought ground itself empty, and at the same time an inclination towards the sensational and wonderful made its appearance, resulting in a literature of its own, paradoxography. Under the early Empire the position was that science brought no new results to light, while the philosophers wrangled over conventional scholastic questions; no guidance was to be found anywhere. A desire for authority and belief seized upon men; with their inborn respect for what was due to age they looked for authorities in the works of ancient times, or else found them in divine revelations. Therefore a high value was set on the immemorial traditional wisdom of the East, in contrast to the Greek itch for discovering novelties. Greek rationalism wasted away as a fire burns itself out for lack of fuel. While science ended in fruitless logomachies and soulless compilations, the religious will to believe got fresh vitality.

The change took place in the middle of the Hellenistic period, about 200 B.C., when the outward helplessness and inner decadence of the Hellenistic States became apparent and crossing between the Greeks and Oriental peoples among whom the Greeks lived had already gone far. The Greeks had got acquainted with the Orientals' conceptions and their wisdom, but they could no longer, as once they had, test and refine them, but content themselves, in accordance with the ruling tendency of that epoch, with working them over and systematizing them. It was then that the astrological system was built up on Babylonian foundations by the help of Greek science; at that same time Bolos of Mendes lived and gave to the conception of power the occult meaning which dominated late antiquity. The conception of force or power had been adopted by science, but since ancient science, unlike modern, could not mark off and measure different forces, power easily got a flavour of something secret and wonderful; it became occult. This conception of occult forces gave a show of justification to magic and sorcery, and at the same time late antiquity reverted to a primitive dynamism.

Religion made science its underling. The so-called science of late antiquity is speculative and mystical and appeals to revelations and dealings with the supernatural world. But, like magic, it always has a practical aim and does not research for the sake of researching. The fundamental idea was the concept of sympathy or antipathy between certain things, plants and beasts, which in turn rests upon dynamism. The analogies with which Greek rationalism worked shot up like weeds in the hothouse of mysticism. There was no longer any difference between religion and science, for both rested upon divine revelation; religion had swallowed science up.

Belief and revelation took the place of research and investigation. To this was added credulity, superstition, and belief in sorcery in an increasing degree, made legitimate by the doctrine of occult forces. In the East, the old belief in the connexion of science with religion had never been broken. The Greeks had always admired the wisdom of the Orient, and now this admiration was strengthened in a fatal manner. In the East, the old unbroken traditions and much that was wonderful were to be found. Therefore the wisdom of the East was appealed to and works published under the names of Oriental sages, Zoroaster, Ostanes, and others; the astrological and alchemical works of Hermes Trismegistos also belong here. These names were letters of recommendation for the works which bore them.

In time, science became in Greece what it had always been in the East, an adjunct of religion. This change is intimately connected with the religious change. For a better understanding of the religious experience of late antiquity it is useful to compare it with similar phenomena in other times, including our own. It moves in the region of mysticism and occultism and its theology is theosophy, which always follows occultism as its theoretical shadow.

As the religion of late antiquity appeared in the forms of mysteries, Hermetism and Gnosticism, and reached its climax in Neoplatonic theurgy, spiritism and theosophy have grown up in our own times from the same soil. In our days this movement excited a great deal of attention, but was exclusively concerned with the other life and the world of spirits, was confined to certain circles, and in time died down. The corresponding tendency in late antiquity was much wider spread, turned its attention to gods and daimones, and rallied the last forces of heathendom to oppose the triumphant advance of Christianity. This intellectual background for the religion of late antiquity is much more important than the question of whence the religious doctrines came, a question to which it is not always possible to give a certain answer. In our time the spiritistic and occult movement was a European phenomenon, which appealed for preference to Indian lore and set up mahatmas as unapproachable models, while the theosophy of late antiquity likewise appealed to the wisdom of the East and to Oriental sages. On unprepared ground, this movement would not have grown so strongly, but the ground had been prepared owing to the general conversion, the longing for something to believe. Old seeds which had lain dormant during the rationalistic drought put forth new shoots, while from the East there came in other elements, which were adopted and developed further.

Mystics have existed in all ages and in all religions. Their characteristic feature is the higher illumination, the attempt to unite themselves with and be absorbed into deity, the *unio mystica*. This attempt finds expression in more than one way. One is the silent rapture, ecstatic contemplation, in which the sense-impressions vanish and the man feels himself exalted to a higher, a divine world. This is the result of silent contemplation, the goal towards which the holy stillness practised by the Neoplatonists and still used by Indian mystics leads. How highly it was prized is shown by its importance in Hermetism and the circumstance that one of the highest Aeons in Gnosticism was Sige, Silence. A similar ecstasy is often produced by self-hypnosis, brought about by the monotonous murmuring of prayers and formulae, such as the Indian *tat tvam asi*. For that very purpose the Neoplatonists highly prized and warmly recommended prayers; the magical papyri are full of prayers to be recited, for the magicians were children of the same spirit and worked with

similar means. The more violent rapture which is expressed
in shouting and bodily movements is akin to the kind we have
described, although mystics as a general rule prefer quieter
forms. Antiquity knew that sort of ecstasy also, for instance
that of the Pythia. In late antiquity it became more general
and served as a means for union with deity. The great expert
in theurgy, Iamblichos the Neoplatonist, describes it in
detail, defends it, and differentiates it from simple madness.

Visions of gods, revelations, apparitions are always and
everywhere experienced by mystics. There is an account in
the Christian collection *Apophthegmata patrum* which is enlightening for the value placed by heathen and Christian
alike on visions of deities and on ascetic practices as a means
of reaching that end. Its simplicity bears an unmistakable
stamp of credibility.

The Abbot Olympios said: There came a priest of the Greeks
(pagans) to Sketis (in Egypt) and entered my cell and slept there;
and having seen the monks' manner of life, he said to me, 'Since you
live thus, have you no visions from your God?' And I said to him,
'No'. And the priest said to me, 'While we perform the holy rites to
our god, he hides nothing from us, but reveals his secrets to us, and
you, who toil so, with vigils, silences and spiritual exercises, do you
tell me that you see no visions? Surely then, if you see none, you have
evil thoughts in your hearts, which sever you from your God, and that
is why He does not reveal His secrets to you.' And I went and told
our elders the words of the priest, and they marvelled and said, 'It is
so, for unclean thoughts sever God from man.'

How much importance late antiquity attached to divine
revelations is shown by the fact that not only religious but
also pseudo-scientific doctrines, alchemy and astrology, are
represented as revelations given by a vision of a god. Knowledge, *gnosis*, is no longer got by mental labour but by
revelation. By *gnosis* is meant a strong religious tendency of
which Christian Gnosticism is a part; Hermetism also is
gnosis, divine revelation, in this sense. Certainly, divine
revelation is a well-worn literary form, but it often appears,

especially among Neoplatonists, that visions really belonged to the religious experience of late antiquity and had an extraordinarily great importance. As early as the second century A.D., sentimental pietists like Aelius Aristides had visions. They play a great part in Hermetic writings and in Iamblichos' work *On the Mysteries*, our most important source for religious feeling in late antiquity. Iamblichos says that the soul receives a new and higher life by contemplating the holy phenomena of theurgy, operates with fresh power, and rightly feels itself more than human. He describes in detail the divine shapes which appear; the theurgist sees the spirit descending. He speaks also of visual and auditory hallucinations which occur in a half-waking state. It is self-evident that such phenomena occurred in magic also, whose endeavour indeed it was to evoke them. Even cheating and conjuring tricks were not shunned, in order to counterfeit them.

To produce such a visionary and ecstatic condition, the mystics of late antiquity used the same means as mystics in other ages and among other peoples—the weakening of the body and dulling of the senses by fasting and ascetic practices. They despised the body, which for them was but a hindrance to the higher illumination. What pious contemplation, holy silence, and prayer meant for them has already been told. The same means, fasting and silence, purifications and the murmuring of long prayers, are found again in apocalyptic writings and magic texts as necessary preparations.

Comprehension of this state of mind is the firmest foundation for comprehending mystical belief and its expressions in Hermetism, Gnosticism, and finally in Neoplatonism and theurgy; the same attitude is found again in Christian mystics of a later date. The feeling of deliverance from the corporeal and exaltation over the earthly which ecstasy produces is the reason why a man no longer thinks of himself as belonging to this earthly region and considers himself reborn as a new and spiritual man, sometimes even exalted to deity; that he believes he is set free from the chain of causality, from *heimarméne*, that he despises what is corporeal, tries to get free from it by means of ascetic practices, and sometimes considers it the root and ground of evil. This elevation is given by *gnosis*, true knowledge of God and the divine, which is got by vision of deity. From this is produced contempt for those who do not possess *gnosis*, cannot have a vision of deity, but are held fast in the fetters of the body. Redemption also is marked by these conceptions in the Hermetic writings. It depends on the sensation which ecstasy gives, of being freed from and exalted above the corporeal and of sharing in the eternal and divine, which mystics experience when in that state. Man passes into deity. This is immortality, but immortality of the soul, not the body, in that it is the spirit which is united to deity.

Occultism is in our day of the same stuff as mysticism, a variety which originates in a tired civilization, like that of late antiquity or our own times, when old belief has failed and superstition flaunts itself in its place and dresses in the forms and thoughts of mysticism. About a generation ago, occultism and theosophy attracted much attention; Madame Blavatsky and Mrs. Annie Besant were names in everyone's mouth and the Society for Psychical Research was founded in Britain. There were some who sought to investigate the curious phenomena which took place; there were some honestly convinced, some who were charlatans and deceivers, while exposures of trickery were not rare. It was the same in late antiquity. Spiritists still apply their art to foretell the future; there are crystal-gazing mediums and sibyls. In late antiquity this was the predominant side of occultism; the majority of the practices described in the magical papyri have divination and nothing else in view. The future was foretold by staring into the flame of a lamp or into a pool of water and in various other ways; occasionally the dead were called back to life. We make a distinction between occultism and spiritism on the one hand, magic and sorcery on the other; the latter is, to us, common superstition and trickery. This distinction is not valid for late antiquity. Ancient magicians applied occult methods; in the magical papyri numerous borrowings from the higher religion are embedded and long, often impressive, prayers are included. It is for that reason that these texts are so important for understanding the religious mentality of the age. We have already mentioned theurgy, the art of evoking apparitions of gods, which the later Neoplatonists made out to be the very crown of religion; it is nothing but magic or sorcery decked out in religion's robes.

Late antique practitioners of theurgy and magic worked with the same means and the same phenomena which appear in modern spiritistic seances, but with certain differences due to the conditions of that time. One of the most discussed is what is known as levitation, that is, that a person, without being affected by any outward cause and independent of the laws of gravitation, becomes lighter, and can sometimes make himself rise into the air; experiments have been devised to test it. Indian fakirs can mount up into the air, and the same is alleged of many saints and is accepted as evidence of sanctity by the Catholic Church. The same thing is told of the Neoplatonic philosopher and theurgist, Iamblichos. He himself speaks of levitation when describing ecstasy. Sorcerers had the same faculty; it is often said that they hovered in the air. There were also appliances completely corresponding to modern apparatus for automatic writing, although they were differently constructed.

Spiritism gets its name from the spirit-revelations which are produced at séances. Practitioners of theurgy and magic in late antiquity also called up spirits. There is indeed the difference that modern spiritists devote their attention to the spirits of the dead, while ancient magicians were concerned with gods and daimones, but that is a difference depending on the circumstances of the times. The ancient polytheism and belief in daimones is now extinct; on the other hand, life after death was not a problem to the ancients, for they entirely believed in it, even though their ideas about it varied. The future interested them more, and spirits, including sometimes ghosts of the dead, were evoked to throw light upon it. In our days spiritistic seances are held in a dimly lighted room; in antiquity the phenomena generally took place in strong light, although darkness was not unknown. Strong light will do as well as darkness to deceive the eyes, especially if they are alternately opened and shut, as was prescribed when magicians were scrying with a lamp-flame. Luminous apparitions (*photismata*) are very often mentioned in the literature dealing with this subject; for instance, Proklos the Neoplatonist was attended by them.

The fact that we conceive the soul as immaterial is a difficulty for the modern spiritists' belief in apparitions of ghosts; it is got rid of by a hypothesis invented for the occasion, materialization as it is called; the souls dress themselves in an 'astral body', in order to be revealed to mortals. This difficulty did not exist for the ancients, who never doubted that gods and daimones, if they wished to, could reveal themselves in perceptible guise. The Neoplatonists had, however, a related though somewhat different hypothesis; the soul was, according to it, clad in an ethereal covering called the *óchema*, and this was illuminated by divine light, so that the apparitions of deities could affect our sensitive faculties.

The trance, brought about by suggestion or self-hypnotism, is one of the most important auxiliaries of modern spiritism for getting into *rapport* with the spirit-world. The person who goes into a trance is called a medium, because he is the intermediary of this *rapport*. The same phenomenon recurs in antiquity, e.g. scrying was done by gazing at the surface of water, a method, by the way, which reminds us of modern crystal-gazing. As medium, an innocent boy was chosen, after his suitability for the purpose had been tested, but anyone who had the gift could carry out the process himself. The medium, with his eyes shut or bandaged, lay on his belly with his face over a vessel containing water. Thereupon certain ceremonies were gone through, which led up to the trance into which the medium passed by staring at the surface of the water, wherein he saw the beings summoned by the magician, and they gave answers to the questions asked.

Frauds and conjuring-tricks of charlatans who have associated themselves to the spiritistic movement are now quite often exposed. It was the same in antiquity likewise. We are informed concerning a Neoplatonist, Maximus, the admired teacher of the Emperor Julian, that he made a statue of Hekate smile and the torches in her hands blaze up. A more intelligent Neoplatonist, Eusebios, warned the future Emperor against his arts, but in vain. It is said concerning Julian himself that at his initiation into the mysteries he was taken down into a subterranean room, where he was at first frightened with horrible noises, revolting smells, and fiery apparitions. Sundry more examples might be given, and it is to be feared that such conjuring-tricks played a considerable part in the mysteries of late antiquity.

The garment of religion in which mystic and occultist phenomena disguised themselves, theosophy, was much less like that of modern times, because it was determined by the religious and philosophical views of the day, and here comes a decided difference between present-day Christianity and ancient polytheism and belief in daimones. Considerations of space prevent us going into details about the subtle Neoplatonic doctrines, but it may just be remarked that in its essence, in its relations to the other world and to the divine, ancient theosophy is substantially the same as modern. Its ideas persisted and drew into their magic circle those whose souls were inclined to mysticism; I have seen an American book about Freemasonry which was full of Neoplatonism. Another resemblance was the appeal to the wisdom of foreign peoples. In our days, theosophists value mahatmas and yoga; their ancient colleagues set store by the sages of the East and their wisdom.

The mystic and occultist current set much stronger in late antiquity than in our own time, for the advance of science keeps it within bounds, investigates the enigmatic phenomena, and tries to comprehend them, especially by a more profound understanding of the night-side of the soul, and exposes trickery and conjuring. In late antiquity, science was dead, and what passed under its name was at the same time occultism and theosophy. Nowadays occultism is confined to quite narrow circles; in late antiquity it was much more widely spread, although the great majority remained unaffected by it. The average man no doubt marvelled at the occult phenomena, as many do even now, and supposed there must be 'something in them'. For him they were something enigmatic, uncanny, and illicit, and he put them on the same plane as sorcery. This was true also of State authorities, for they, not without reason, included theurgy under the prohibition against sorcery, since theurgy was at the same time occultist magic. For most people, occult phenomena were something secret and dangerous, against which they tried to protect themselves, and theosophy was much too high-flown speculation.

This side of the later religion of antiquity has received but scanty attention from the researchers of recent years, in comparison with the much-discussed mystery religions, to which we shall come in the next section; perhaps it has been felt that it belongs to so late a period that it has not much importance for religious development. However, theurgy is quite old; the founder of it, a certain Julianus, who composed the abstruse oracles known as Chaldaean, lived under Marcus Aurelius, and the art of scrying and seeing visions on the surface of water with the help of a medium is mentioned as early as Varro, in the first century B.C. The emotional character of the mysteries leads to a suspicion that similar

phenomena had long occurred in them; we shall see in
the next section that such things were abundant towards
the close of antiquity. Furthermore, we must not neglect the
great importance such matters had in magic. The later
Neoplatonists adopted and developed these phenomena and
these arts, because they furnished a substitute for the
mystical rapture which but few could experience, and that
not often; this explains the overwhelming importance they
attached to theurgy. We really cannot properly understand
the religious feeling of late antiquity without taking occultism
into account. It was in a way the vulgar form of transcendentalism, even though the Neoplatonists tried to
dignify it with theosophical speculation.

8. THE MYSTERY-RELIGIONS

Ever since the end of last century, the mysteries have
been in the forefront of interest in researches touching the
religion of late antiquity, and to them must be added the
mystical forms of religion to be found in certain writings—
sometimes they are spoken of as book-mysteries. Both may
be taken together as mystery-religions. From the frag-
mentary information, hard as it is to interpret, which we
have about the mysteries and their rites, attempts have been
made to construct a mystery-theology showing an affinity
to Christianity, and from the mystery-religions some have
tried to prove a terminology of mysteries, which they have
found again in Christian works, amongst others those of
St. Paul, without observing the necessity of an exact comparison with non-religious linguistic usage, or remembering
that Greek, even in scientific works, lacked a fixed terminology as exact as those with which we are familiar.

The most important of the mystical book-religions,
Hermetism and Gnosticism, have been treated in a previous
section; in the present section we will examine the mysteries
and the aforesaid mystery-theology in their connexion with
the chief currents of religious feeling expounded earlier.

This short account does not attempt a discussion of the several
mysteries and their rites, such as would inevitably be com-
prised in a thoroughgoing treatment of the documentation,
which is often obscure and controversial. It touches merely
upon the chief features of the essence of the mysteries, in so
far as they throw light upon religious feeling.

The most important mysteries were of foreign origin and
had arisen in the cult of certain gods, Isis, the Great Mother
(with Attis), Sabazios, and Mithra. Of these, Mithra passed
Greece by, and in the East, even in Asia Minor, the traces of
his mysteries are very faint. The mysteries of Attis were of
most importance in the western parts of the Empire, where
they were to some extent organized as part of the Roman
State cult. The goddess who was incomparably the most
zealously worshipped by the Greeks and whose mysteries were
the most important for them was Isis. Sabazios was a deity
akin to Dionysos, but of less account; he was worshipped in
certain regions of Asia Minor. Dionysos' numerous mysteries
attached themselves to the old Greek cults. To these mysteries
we must add Neoplatonic theurgy, which towards the end
of antiquity passed into mysteries.

The religious ideas which are said to lie at the bottom of
the mysteries—what has been spoken of above as mystery-
theology—can be summed up in a few words: death and
resurrection, regeneration and sonship of God, enlightenment and redemption, deification and immortality. We must
examine the importance and extent of these conceptions in
the mysteries.

Death is merely the first act, which is necessarily followed
by resurrection. When death is mentioned in the mysteries,
it appears that it was an image or metaphor, signifying the
complete break with the earlier, rejected life which initiates
into the mysteries made, as those received into a monastic
order in Christendom sometimes do under similar forms.
The most important point, however, is the conception that,
as the god dies and rises again, so the initiate shall also die

and rise again. But this is contradicted by the myths which are associated with the mysteries. Attis was and remained dead. Osiris' limbs were collected and he rose, but only to be ruler over the kingdom of the dead. However, it is undeniable that the thought of death, departure, and the return of life had a place in these two old vegetation-cults. The immortality which the magician tries to gain in the papyrus text which is wrongly called the Mithra-liturgy aims at getting predictions concerning the future and lasts only as long as the magical process goes on; when that is finished, the magician resumes his human nature.

The words which signify 'to be born again' (*renasci, palingenesia*, &c.) are often employed, even in common speech, with a metaphorical meaning. In the mysteries of Isis the entry upon a new career in life which the initiate accomplished is described as a rebirth, and he who was cleansed from his pollutions by the baptism of blood in the taurobolium began a new life and was said to be reborn; the day on which he received this bloody baptism was said to be his birthday. Words with the same significance are used to describe vividly a man's transition from his earlier condition, which he abandons, to the higher one which he reaches by initiation into mysteries. This is rather an interpretation of the rites than an idea from which the rites originated.

When a man is reborn by the grace of God, he can be called the child of God, a description which is familiar in Christianity but not found in the mysteries. The roundabout ways in which it has been attempted to prove that such a conception did exist in the mysteries do not lead to their goal, and the evidence produced is of no importance. In paganism, God or the gods are said often to be the father or fathers of mankind, but not that men are the children of God, whom He receives into His mercy. The great achievement of Christianity is that it interpreted the fatherhood of God in this way and so made man's sonship to God a focal point of its belief.

Salvation is for us a theological idea, which Christian literature describes as a deliverance, *apolýtrosis*, the freeing of man from his sins and the eternal death which is their wages, by the blood of Christ. This can also be called *soteria*, using a word belonging to everyday speech and meaning rescue; but only the religious tendency of the context can introduce a deeper meaning into that word. The purifications which preluded initiation into the mysteries had no other object than to efface the impurities clinging to the candidate for initiation; the aim of the mysteries, to assure the initiate a blessed life in the other world, was a deliverance from its terrors. But all this fails to touch the kernel of the matter. The real salvation which the mysteries offered was salvation from *heimarméne*, from unavoidable destiny. This is the principal theme in Apuleius' account of the mysteries of Isis; Hermetism taught that he who knows God is free from *heimarméne*, and the journey to the highest heaven was signified by symbols in the mysteries of Mithra. This salvation is the fundamental idea in Gnosticism, where it is attained by the higher illumination, whereas for the Church illumination is belief. The doctrine of salvation in the mysteries has its roots in cosmological speculations which were attached to the conception of the universe, whereas that of Christianity is purely religious.

That a human being may become a god was well known in ancient paganism; we have only to remember the worship of kings. However, to prove that such a conception exists in the mysteries, we must once more go by roundabout routes. Sexual union is represented as an image of union with God. Mythology furnished plentiful examples of a god choosing a mortal bride, and it really occurred in Oriental religions; but the proof offered for the existence of such a rite in the mysteries is insufficient. The words in the sacred formula of the mysteries of Attis which are commonly translated 'I entered the bridal chamber' really mean 'I entered the Holy of Holies of the temple'. The snake which was drawn through the bosom in the mysteries of Sabazios is not a phallic symbol; the object of the rite was to impart divine strength to the initiand by contact with the god, thought of as in serpent-form. The existence of sexual symbols with this significance in the Eleusinian Mysteries is an unproved hypothesis, sprung from the predilection for such rites and interpretations which certain researchers cherish. Coarse images borrowed from sexual life are not unusual, but pagan parallels to the familiar conception of Christ as the Bridegroom and the Church as the Bride are scarcely to be found. That passes over to the holy virgins who vowed everlasting chastity and sometimes sought satisfaction in sensually warm imagery; but paganism had no hysterical nuns and mysticism was practised by men.

The sacramental meal or communion did not make a human being into a god but gave him a share in divine potency. It is found in the old cults and naturally in the mysteries. In those of Mithra the mystic was served with bread and water; the prototype was perhaps the banquet which Mithra and the sun-god shared. We know equally little of the ceremony in the mysteries of Attis at which the mystic ate and drank from the sacred utensils, hand-drums and cymbals, but assuredly a communion took place in both these rites, by means of which the mystic received a share of the divine potency; an idea which was supported by the pre-vailing belief in potency.

So much is talked about immortality that we must be clear as to what immortality really is. Immortality of the body, the resurrection of the flesh, was rejected by paganism. That the soul is immortal is a primeval belief, much blended with corporeal conceptions. The soul was thought of in a more or less corporeal form and passed either into a blissful life in the other world, which was described in very material colours, or else to purification and punishment, which was painted in a no less material way. In late antiquity the material conceptions were more and more attenuated (for instance, the purifications and punishments were transferred to the atmosphere) until they were completely rejected in Hermetism, which transformed the soul into pure potency. Immortality is nothing new; the novelty is that while the older belief made the transition from earthly to eternal life take place at death, the mysteries transferred it to the moment of initiation. In this way the immortal life which bestowed happiness in the other world upon the initiate did not wait until death to begin. The immortality which the mysteries gave consisted, *ipso facto*, in the commencement of the blessed other life while the earthly life was still going on, to continue after this life was ended.

Although both paganism and Christianity firmly believed in a life after death, their respective attitudes towards death and immortality were essentially different. The pagan was resigned in face of death; the Christian kicked against the pricks, and broke them. For the pagan, death was the inevitable end of human life; for the Christian, it was essentially an evil, the wages of sin. The pagan feared the empty shadow-life in Hades which followed death, or punishment for the wrongs he had done. The Christian was certain of happiness in the other life, if he repented and turned; for him, immortality was a life fully corporeal, although in a glorified body; punishment threatened sinners, deniers of God and enemies of 'righteousness', i.e., of Christianity. Christianity replaced the everlasting night of pagan poets with everlasting light (*lux aeterna* for *nox aeterna*). The resurrection of the body was unintelligible to the pagan; to him it was self-evident that the body decays in death. To him, immortality was the immortality of the soul, even if the soul was portrayed with material features, and to achieve it was either to live the blessed life in the other world which initiation into the mysteries assured him, or else the union of the soul with the Supreme Being which was the climax of Hermetic and Neoplatonic religion.

An unprejudiced examination of our evidence shows that it is not sufficient for the construction of a mystery-theology.

The dissimilarities between the cults from which the mysteries arose and whose stamp they bore are overlooked or under-estimated. There are certain resemblances between them, such as may be found at earlier times and among other peoples, but no more. There is a like neglect of the dubious quality of our evidence, the vast majority of which comes from Christian writers. These follow two main lines. One is to pick out the most repellent rites and myths, to show the detestability of paganism, the other, to represent the ritual of the mysteries as aping that of Christianity, an attempt of Satan to mislead mankind. It looks almost as if in looking for a mystery-theology the same line was followed, only in the reverse direction. From the notices in Christian writers rites and articles of belief are constructed, which it is then found that Christianity borrowed. Are we not to recognize the gift of originality possessed by Christianity and particularly by St. Paul, one of the greatest religious geniuses that ever lived? He conceived wide ranges of fruitful thought, gave them depth, and created ideas which had the power to grip the religious consciousness not only of antiquity but of all times to come. For its victorious religious power Christianity need not thank the circumstance that it moved along lines travelled by the mystery-religions.

The greatest blunder made in these researches into the secrets of the mysteries is to forget the wise saying of Aristotle, that those who are initiated into them learn nothing but are put into a certain receptive disposition. The emotional element in the human soul is the foundation of the mysteries, and it was upon that that the cults within which they arose constructed them. Aristotle knew more about the mysteries of his own day than we do, and the same note is sounded by later authors when they mention mysteries. Dion Chrysostom describes how he who is brought into the hall of the mysteries sees many mystic sights and hears the like sounds, with alternating appearances of darkness and light; and he adds that he is moved and supposes that all this has some deeper meaning. Two and a half centuries later the rhetorician Themistios gives a similar description which is often, against tradition and without adequate cause, ascribed to Plutarch, who uses similar expressions. The soul of one near death, says the rhetorician, has a like experience to that of an initiate into the mysteries. First come wanderings and wearisome hurryings to and fro in the dark, then, just before the climax, profound fear and apprehension. Then there shines a marvellous light, and pure meadows are revealed, where reverend sounds and words and holy appearances greet him. We may also remember Celsus' comparison of the torments of the Christian Hell with the fearsome representations in the mysteries of Dionysos.

We can but conjecture by what means such a profound emotional effect was produced; we catch a glimpse of them in the famous description of the mysteries of Isis in Apuleius:

I drew near the borders of death; when I had set my foot upon the threshold of Proserpina I returned, carried through all the elements; in the middle of the night I beheld the clear radiance of the sun; I approached the gods both infernal and celestial and worshipped them face to face.

All this cannot be, as some have maintained, mere hallucination, although we certainly must allow for something of the sort playing a considerable part in the mystical appearances. When the mysteries developed under the predominant influence of Neoplatonism, artificial means were employed, if they had not been in use already, to arouse and reinforce the effects aimed at; something will be said of them in the following section. At that period, the highest mysteries, repeatedly mentioned by Proklos, were theurgy. He tells us that in the holiest initiations, before the appearance (*parousía*) of the gods there appear symbols of certain chthonian daimones, which try to confuse the initiands and distract them from the immaculate good. Elsewhere he adds that the mystics at first meet multiform classes of gods sent in advance, but afterwards, upheld and guarded by the rites, receive the divine irradiation.

This is clearly theurgy, as may be seen by comparing the account in Iamblichos' work *On the Mysteries* of the subordinate powers which appear before the *parousia* of the gods; but an unbroken line leads from the account in Dion to that in Proklos. Neoplatonic theurgy, which took a hand in the mysteries in the fourth century A.D., when the champions of paganism were having themselves initiated into as many as possible, developed and strengthened by its arts the means by which it was sought to arouse the initiands' emotions. This emotional basis is prominent even in the older and different mysteries; as early as those of Eleusis, the feelings were roused, as in the later rites, by preliminary purifications and fasting, while the sheen of torches and certain ceremonies about which we are insufficiently informed brought the excitement to its climax. In the mysteries of Mithra there were preliminary tests; in those of Attis, ecstatic dancing to the sound of hand-drums and cymbals, until the novices brought the god the supreme sacrifice by castrating themselves. In those of Isis the ecstasy was less violent, but it is evident enough in Apuleius' account. The Neoplatonists, when they tried by all sorts of artifices to intensify the excitement of emotion, at the same time brought the mysteries to their downfall.

Plutarch bears witness that instruction was given in the mysteries, and Dion Chrysostom speaks of interpreters. If we wish to form an idea of the nature and content of these instructions and explanations, we must not let ourselves be led by modern hypotheses but keep to what the ancients thought about it.

Foremost of all was the allegorical interpretation of rites and myths, which was so flexible and fanciful that it could find room for almost anything under its broad mantle. When the Empire began, it was already half a millennium old; it dominated the philosophical explanations of religion and was applied to the Jewish and Christian Scriptures to an extent incomprehensible to us; it reached its climax with the Neo-platonists. It is true that, because of the secrecy with which the mysteries were surrounded, we are denied any knowledge of how allegorical interpretation explained their rites; but we have good information regarding the myths which belong to the mystery-cults. We can, for instance, read the Emperor Julian's speech *To the Great Mother*, or the little work *On the Gods and the Universe* which was written by his friend Sallustius and has, not unjustly, been styled a Neoplatonic catechism. He interprets the myth of Attis and the great public festival which was celebrated with particular brilliance in Rome at the spring equinox, as follows:

They say that when Attis was lying beside the river Gallos the Mother of the Gods saw him and fell in love with him, and that she took the starry cap and set it on his head and thereafter kept him with her. But he, falling in love with a [water-]nymph, left the Mother of the Gods and lived with the nymph. For this reason the Mother of the Gods drove Attis mad, and he cut off his privy parts and left them with the nymph, afterwards returning and living with Mother again. Now the Mother of the Gods is a life-producing goddess, which is why she is called Mother, while Attis is the creator of things which come into and pass out of existence, and that is why he is said to have been found beside the river Gallos, for the name Gallos riddlingly signifies the Galaxy or Milky Way, which is the [upper] boundary of what is affectible and corporeal. The primary gods perfect the secondary, hence the Mother loves Attis and gives him celestial potencies (that is what the cap means), but Attis loves the nymph; nymphs are the guardians of coming into being, for all that does so is in flux. But, since coming into being must stop some-where, lest its inferior products should be of the very lowest kind, the creator who makes such things leaves his generative potencies with the process of becoming and rejoins the gods. All this never happened, but always is, and mind sees everything at once, while language utters some things first, others afterwards. Since, then, the myth fits the ordered universe, we, in imitation of the universe (for how better could we become ordered ?), consequently keep our feast. First of all, as though we ourselves had fallen from heaven and were in the nymph's company, we are in dejection and abstain from bread and other fattening and impure foods, since both are inimical to the soul. Next come the cutting of the tree and a fast, as though we too were cutting off the further procession of generation; thereupon follows a diet of milk, as if we were reborn. After all this come rejoicings, garlands, and as it were a return to the height of the gods. The occasion of these ceremonies bears further witness to what I have said, for they are performed about the time of the vernal equinox, when things stop coming into being and the day gets longer than the night, which is suitable for the ascent of souls.

In this manner, higher religious and philosophical ideas could be read into the repulsive myth of Attis and the ceremonies which were carried out at his festival. All probability is on the side of supposing like interpretations for the mysteries which inherited myths and rites from the cults.

The other predominant method of interpretation was the cosmological, which leaves its traces even in Sallustius' pronouncements. It attached itself to the current view of the universe and appears in all the mysteries—the ascent of the soul in Hermetism and the mysteries of Mithra, the journey through the elements which the initiate into the mysteries of Isis underwent, and the Phrygian cap with its ornament of stars which Attis wore. A neglected notice, derived from a good source, Porphyry, informs us that in the Eleusinian Mysteries the hierophant appeared in the costume of the Creator, the daduchos as Helios, the priest of the altar as Selene, and the sacred herald as Hermes; this extraordinary statement can be understood only as an interpretation of the richly embroidered robes which these priests had worn from ancient days.

By way of proof of the significance which this line of thought had for the mysteries, we may mention a mystic oath, whose importance is shown by its being preserved on one papyrus from the first and another from the third century A.D. It tells us, of course, nothing of the content of the mysteries, but it is enlightening to observe that it is taken by the creator-god who separated earth from heaven, light from darkness, day from night; rising from setting (of the heavenly bodies), life from death, black from white, dry from moist, fiery from cold, bitter from sweet, and body from soul.

The mysteries did not take the foremost place in shaping the religion of late antiquity which some have wished to ascribe to them; they are rather a symptom of the religious development than its pioneers. We must not forget that the circle of initiates was limited and that they were forbidden to talk about their ritual and doctrine; possibly it might be done in general terms, as, for example, in Apuleius. But that is not enough to give the mysteries the overwhelming influence with which they are credited. To produce such an effect needs an agitation, a mission which appeals to the generality of the people, like that which St. Paul carried out. Much more important than the mysteries were the generally accepted religious ideas which seemed a matter of course to that age, and of which the mysteries are only one expression. The mysteries did not create but adopted these ideas. This religious atmosphere was in itself syncretistic. The form of the mysteries is Greek, modelled upon the secret cults which had existed in Greece since ancient times and of which the Eleusinian Mysteries are the most famous. The mysteries were created by Greeks and half-Greeks in connexion with foreign cults and adopted the contemporary allegorical interpretations and cosmological ideas, the beliefs in power and in daimones. The new mystery-cults, with the exception of that of Dionysos, all belonged to foreign deities, and their content to the religious concepts and speculations of late antiquity, which were also introduced into the ancient mysteries of Greece.

9. FOLK-BELIEF

It may perhaps seem strange that in a book on religious feeling a section should be devoted to folk-belief, superstition, and sorcery, but superstition is the shadow of religion, a weed which draws its nourishment from the same soil; in other words, our justification for taking superstition into account is the light which it throws on the mentality of the age and its intellectual atmosphere. At a time when simple, clear lines of thought are in favour, superstition shrinks into its covert; so it was in the last century, and so it was in the classical age of Greece. But superstition does not die; it merely bides its time and spreads abroad again when the mental atmosphere changes and becomes favourable to it.

Superstition and sorcery, charms and conjurations are all to be found in classical antiquity, but the Greeks felt a dislike towards them; it is significant that the two famous witches of mythology, Kirke and Medeia, are foreign women and that the goddess of ghosts, Hekate, comes from Karia in the south-western corner of Asia Minor. Her triple image was set up in front of house-doors to keep off evil and witchcraft. It is equally significant that Hekate became the favourite deity of magicians and theurgists and in the last age of antiquity had famous mysteries on Aigina. Attempts to harm enemies by sorcery were not lacking. From the Athens of Plato and Demosthenes there has come to light a large number of curse-tablets, as they are called, scraps of lead which were dropped into tombs and on which were scratched conjurations against enemies, who were delivered over to the power of the infernal deities; in late antiquity these are extremely common. As always, charms and conjurations, amulets and magical methods took a leading place in folk-medicine, and diseases were ascribed to supernatural powers. One of the brightest pages of classical culture is the warfare waged by Hippokrates and those of like mind with him against this deep-rooted superstition, and their struggle, inspired by warm conviction, to explain all illnesses by natural causes. The older Hellenistic period adopted the same attitude towards superstition and sorcery. They existed and were popular, but were not received in good society. This is shown by the mentions of them in New Comedy and in Theokritos; the latter's poem concerning a deserted girl who, wavering between hate and affection, uses magical arts against her false lover, is a masterpiece of its kind.

The sharpest contrast between the classical period and late antiquity is in the increasing spread of superstition and sorcery during the latter; the mentality of the age had changed fundamentally, an alteration which may be seen also in its predilection for marvellous stories. Out of Plutarch's works an abundant collection can be made of references to sorcery and magical materials, love-philtres, conjurations, the Evil Eye, amulets, magic wheels, and magical symbols, the so-called Ephesian letters. Apuleius was accused of winning by sorcery the hand of a rich widow, and his defence is still extant. There is an extensive literature on *materia magica* or objects used in sorcery; it includes beasts, plants, stones, metals, parts of the human body, especially the bodies of suicides and of executed criminals, whose wonderful efficacy was ascribed to sympathy and antipathy, legitimized by the belief in power and often connected with astrological speculations.

Lucian has left us a work entitled *The Liar*, a miscellaneous collection of marvellous tales, for instance how a Babylonian wizard brought together all the snakes on an estate and destroyed them, flew through the air, walked on water, and called up a dead man; how a Syrian cured an epileptic by driving the evil spirit out of him and an Arab made a present of a ring fashioned from a cross-nail and also taught a conjuration full of names of power. One of the company tells from his own experience a tale of the same kind, familiar also in our day, of a house in which someone who had been murdered and buried under the floor 'walked' and haunted the place. The merriest tale of all is that which Goethe used in *Der Zauberlehrling* and Barham for the story of Lay-Brother Peter and the broomstick. A wizard's apprentice had overheard his master's conjurations and with the help of them made a pestle fetch water, but as he had not learned the spell which would force the pestle to stop, the house was flooded with water; he chopped the pestle in two, which continued to fetch water, each piece by itself, until his master arrived and put an end to his troubles with the correct spell. The point of the satire is that these nursery tales are told in a circle of philosophers and educated men, who repose implicit belief in them. Lucian's satire was helpless against the prevailing spirit of the age.

The same author gives a fantastic description of the Elysian Fields, but oftener and with greater zest he paints Hell in the most gloomy colours. The educated regarded these imaginations as mere fable, but they had a serious basis; even Plutarch, to say nothing of the Sibylline oracles, has sadistic descriptions of the torments of the damned. The old belief in a place of punishment in the nether world was embroidered with fancies increasingly gruesome. Its survival was helped by the cult of the dead, which continued to be practised in the old fashion; the custom of bringing food and drink to the graves and having meals at them was taken over by the Church and has continued in the Balkans down to our own day. The numerous sarcophagi which portray the wild following of Dionysos point to the way in which happiness in the next world was pictured. Magicians called up the dead by their spells and used pieces of corpses as powerful means to their sorceries. The ideas concerning the flight of the soul to heaven which we have mentioned above were not shared by the multitude, which for its part believed that the souls of the pious went up to the sky and gathered around the throne of God. Conceptions of the other life grew continually more concrete and punishments were thought of no longer as a means of purifying the wrongdoer but as revenge. There is no denying that Hell is a Greek invention, but Christianity introduced the fateful change that instead of offences against good morals unbelief was made the reason for damnation. This belief and its development are treated at greater length in my Swedish book on *Punishment and Felicity in the Other World in Pre-Christian Religion.*

The Greeks of all periods believed most firmly in dreams which foretold the future, while signs and omens are important even in one of the older historians, such as Herodotos. In late antiquity this sort of thing increased more and more. The historian Cassius Dio, who was a highly educated man and occupied the chief posts in the Roman civil service, came first before the public with a work on the dreams and portents which moved Septimius Severus to aspire to the purple, and afterwards, encouraged by dreams, composed a history of the Emperor Commodus. After he conceived the idea of his great historical work, he was upheld in his task by dreams. Artemidoros of Daldis used the extensive older literature on the interpretation of dreams to make his dreambook, and added to it from his own experience. The *Historia Augusta* often relates signs and wonders, and many Emperors shared the belief of their times. Ammianus Marcellinus tells us of terrible portents, says that such things quite often occur, and laments that they frequently do not become known, because they are no longer expiated after the ancient Roman fashion.

Still more significant for the spirit of that age are the accounts which the same historian gives of the unhappy consequences of superstition; in his day special attention was called to these on account of the Emperor Constantius' suspicious nature. Sorcery and theurgy were made punishable and it was a capital offence to learn by the aid of an oracle how long the reigning Emperor was to live and who should be his successor. In the year A.D. 359 some of the questions which were asked at the oracle of the god Bes in Upper Egypt and of the answers given to them came to the Emperor's knowledge. The result was a great trial during which many were tortured and the result was the capital punishment of some. This went so far, Ammianus adds, that if anyone wore an amulet around his neck to guard against

ague or some other illness, or if he passed a tomb in the
twilight, he was taxed with being a poisoner (*ueneficus*, i.e. a
wizard) and collecting horrible materials from the graves
and the ghosts who wandered about them, and so condemned
to death. Barbatio, the general officer commanding the
cavalry, was executed because his wife was persuaded that a
swarm of bees settling on his house might mean that he had
hopes of the purple. The ever-threatening danger of death
could not stifle curiosity. In the reign of the Emperor Valens
certain prominent men tried, with the help of a sort of ouija-
board, to discover who should be his successor. They took
a metal basin, around the rim of which were engraved the
letters of the alphabet; with great and complicated ceremony, one of them held a ring hanging from a thread over
the basin, and the ring, moving, swung towards the rim,
sometimes at one point and sometimes at another. The
letters THEO were read off and the inference immediately
drawn that a high official named Theodoros was to be the
fortunate one. Both he and many others were tortured and
executed. These are but a few examples out of many.

It is said that under the Empire the oracles lost their
reputation and ceased. This is true only to a certain extent;
there were famous oracles, and new ones came into being,
for instance Alexandros' oracle at Abonuteichos in Asia
Minor, of which Lucian gives a venomous description. Belief
in oracles increased and extended, but there were now simpler
ways of foretelling the future, which could be employed at
any time and anywhere, and some of them by anyone, while
others needed the co-operation of a man skilled in such arts,
a magician, of whom there was never any lack. The simplest
procedure was to throw two or three dice and then look at
a list to see what the throw meant. Counters, grain, or flour
might be spread out, and these were at times somehow set
in motion, for Iamblichos tells us that the divine potency
instils soul into lifeless matter and movement into the motion-
less, for instance pebbles, sticks, grains of corn, or flour.

Magicians scryed by the flame of a lamp. After muttering long prayers with the eyes alternately open and shut, the operator would see the flame shape itself into a room; when he had prayed again with the eyes shut, he could see on opening them that everything was enlarged and brilliantly illuminated. The opening and shutting of the eyes was well adapted to produce sensory illusions. They might also scry by gazing at a white wall covered with mysterious symbols. The method of seeing visions on the surface of water has been described in an earlier section.

The belief in amulets is ineradicable. Your purse has perhaps a lucky penny in it, and such very up-to-date gentry as motorists and airmen carry mascots. There have always been amulets, but belief in and use of them increased under the Empire in an unheard-of manner. Precious stones and their virtues were described in special works, of which one is preserved among the poems ascribed to Orpheus. It begins with an assurance that Hermes has given mankind means of protection against all evil; some protect against wild beasts and brigands, others provide kings with power and honour among foreign peoples, others make slaves faithful to their masters, others bring girls to the beds of young men. Various kinds of precious and semi-precious stones had various virtues; our museums possess quantities of engraved stones with inscriptions and figures which filled them with potency. Of these, some are known as Gnostic gems owing to the peculiarities of their inscriptions and designs. Superstition was an amazingly wide and shifting field, which included all objects, beasts and plants, all the occupations and businesses of life. It is not possible to go into detail, but it may be remarked that the agricultural treatises from late antiquity are full of such recipes. And once again we may remind ourselves that all this superstition was legitimized by the belief in potencies.

Obviously, statues of gods were fuller of potency than amulets. In the classical period, the miracles ascribed to such statues were very modest, generally omens. Many rejected the use of images in worship, among them Xenophanes, and in the second century A.D. certain philosophers still spoke quite contemptuously of them, but the belief in their marvellous power spread. It would seem that a statue might through some accidental cause win the reputation of being miracle-working. It is recorded that one of the many statues of Neryllinos, proconsul of Asia Minor under the Emperor Vespasian, gave oracles and healed the sick. Lucian has two stories of statues in his work *The Liar*, already mentioned. One of them represented a Corinthian general, Pelichos. Every night it walked about the house and often bathed; it was hung with ribbons and garlands and its chest was covered with gold-leaf, and it was customary to lay coins on the pedestal or fasten them to the thigh of the statue with wax as offerings and by way of thanks for being cured of fever. Once when a slave stole some of these coins, he could not find his way out and was caught and soundly thrashed.

The description is grotesque, but it contains details taken from reality; statues were worshipped, money offered to them, and garlands and ribbons hung on them. We are not without information about a cult of images reminding us of that which can still be found in the Catholic countries of southern Europe. Philostratos says that a statue of the hero Protesilaos was worn away from being anointed and having written prayers attached to it. The cult of images in late antiquity is strikingly illustrated by an anecdote concerning the celebrated rhetorician Proairesios; in their enthusiasm many licked his chest as if he were an image filled with divine potency, and kissed his hands, we are told.

Dion Chrysostom goes to the root of the human desire to worship images:

By reason of their eagerness for the divine, all men have a strong impulse to honour and serve deity close at hand, bringing offerings and garlands. Most like to little children torn from father or mother, who are filled with strange longing and wistfulness and often in their dreams stretch out their arms to their absent parents, so men—and rightly, because of their beneficence and their kinship to us—in their love for the gods seek in every way to be with them and in their company.

But many worshipped images purely and simply because they considered them full of divine potency. Even the philosopher Plotinos acquiesced in that doctrine.

Since by the law of sympathy like is attracted to like [he says in effect], so the higher potencies also are participated by preference by what resembles them. When the image of a particular god is fashioned according to the idea of him, it is connected with that god through that idea in the same way as sensible objects in general are connected with intelligibles through the soul. Even though the god does not inhabit the image, yet his potency, which is given out from him to the sensible world, does inhabit the image in a peculiar way.

The old objection, which the Christians took up, that images were nothing but dead matter, wood, stone, or metal, was met by the doctrine that they were filled with divine potency. Iamblichos wrote a work, now lost, on that subject. As amulets could be charged with potency by magical ceremonies, so, according to the opinion of that age, could divine potency be called down into the image of a god in a similar fashion. A Christian author represents a pagan as saying that the pagans do not regard metal or stone as gods or divine powers, but worship the gods whom the holy act of dedication has called down into the images made by human hands and induced to take up their abode in them, and this often occurs. Finally, we may remember the 'philosopher' Heraïskos, already mentioned, who passed into an ecstasy when he caught sight of a 'living' image, but was unaffected if the image lacked potency.

A living man could, like an image, be filled with divine power. The Greek men of God (theioi andres), of whom Apollonios of Tyana is the most celebrated, were at least half philosophers; they proclaimed a higher conception of God, a better morality, and a righteous and strict way of life; but they likewise worked miracles, healed the sick, now and then raised the dead, and appeared suddenly in distant places. Numerous legends gathered around them, and there were some who knew how to turn the people's honest belief into hard cash, for instance Alexandros of Abonuteichos. The Greeks admired the sages of distant lands, Indian Brahmans and Ethiopian gymnosophists. Plutarch has a marvellous story of a sage who lived by the Red Sea and met human beings only once a year, spending the rest of his time in the company of nymphs and daimones; he took nourishment only once a month, and that was a bitter herb. When he prophesied once a year, princes and their secretaries gathered about him. Celsus, in his controversial work against the Christians, mentions prophets in Palestine and Phoenicia who said they were gods or sons of a god or of the divine spirit; they preached repentance and reformation and the approaching end of the world, and praised those who followed after salvation.

The later Neoplatonists were men of God of this kind. Iamblichos was always called 'the divine' by his disciples. Concerning Proklos we are informed that day and night he practised Chaldean incantations, purifications, and expiations and magic circles and consorted with luminous phantoms of Hekate; once while he was lecturing, his head was seen to be encircled with radiance. He freed Athens from drought and from an earthquake and had learned the means of consorting with gods, the theurgic art, from Asklepigeneia, the daughter of Nestorios the reviver of Neoplatonism in Athens. The heading of this section promised a discussion of folk-belief, but now we find ourselves among philosophers. But the later Neoplatonists were in agreement with folk-belief and their religion was in practice magic and the Black Art.

10. THE DAEMONIZING OF RELIGION

A conception in which philosophy and folk-belief joined hands was the belief in daimones. It has been mentioned earlier that the philosopher Xenokrates constructed this doctrine on the basis of certain utterances of Plato. It was eagerly received; Plutarch is of the opinion that it is one of the greatest advances made by philosophy. Celsus defended it and emphasized that daimones are everywhere present. According to the philosophers, Maximus of Tyre, the Neopythagoreans, and the Neoplatonists, the world swarms with them. Daimones filled the gap lying between gods and humanity, as mediators and intermediate beings, who had a kind of more subtle bodies and did not lack human defects and passions; some of them were good, others evil. They also filled the gap in the cosmology between earth, the habitation of men, and the superlunary world, which is populated by gods; their abode was the air beneath the moon, but it was by no means forgotten that they also wandered about the earth and most especially in the neighbourhood of tombs. As the gods were deposed from the highest place by reason of the conception of a one and only supreme God, ruler of everything and everyone, they came dangerously near the daimones, an idea which Christianity followed to its logical consequence by transforming heathen gods into evil daimones.

The doctrine of daimones is connected with that concerning power. Antiquity could not imagine an abstract force with no starting-point; potency was to be found in objects, statues, amulets, and so on, but especially belonged to gods and daimones. The Greek deities had long lost their marvellous powers and lost ground in folk-belief, all except Hekate the witch-goddess and Asklepios the god of healing. But the daimones, whose importance continually increased and who were credited with supernatural interventions in human life on the widest scale, possessed precisely that supernatural potency which was believed in; their names and pictures flood the magical papyri and the amulets. The result of this connexion was that religion was, so to say, daemonized more and more, and this is a conspicuous phenomenon in the religion of late antiquity.

Belief in daimones found a *point d'appui* in the belief in ghosts, which was not lacking in ancient Greece, although it was banished to the nursery and the lower levels of folk-belief. Such bogies as Empusa and Lamia, which are still not forgotten in modern Greek folk-lore, were not indeed called daimones, but as early as the fourth century B.C. the word daimon was so deteriorating that it was used especially in connexion with unlucky happenings; for once belief in daimones became prevalent, the evil daimones came to the fore and when finally Christianity treated the pagan gods as evil daimones, the word got the meaning which 'demon' has in modern speech. Because of the ambiguous position of the daimones it has been necessary, in order to avoid misunderstanding, to use the word here in its Greek form, *daimon*.

Madness and insanity, in the archaic Greek period, were explained by supposing the patient to be possessed by some god, or still more often by nymphs. In late antiquity possession was ascribed as a matter of course to daimones. Lucian speaks of a Syrian wizard who expelled daimones from an epileptic; Egyptian magicians and Apollonios of Tyana cast out evil spirits from people; the magical papyri have formulae for that purpose and a certain stone, if worn in a finger-ring, would put daimones to flight.

In Homer, the word *daimon* means a god or the unknown power which sends a particular happening; but the word was degenerating, for in Plato the daimones appear as intermediate beings between gods and human beings, whence Xenokrates developed his doctrine concerning them. As the old gods lost their power and were no longer the objects of a living faith, the way was open for the daimones. The belief in them found its foothold in the old belief in apparitions and was strongly reinforced by Oriental influence. For in the East, belief in such powers flourished; Babylonian and Egyptian sorcerers enjoyed a high reputation for the Black Art, and they brought their gods and daimones with them, all of whom were particularly potent. Belief in magic and daimones arose out of the depths of the people as a reaction against Greek anthropomorphism, both in its outward form, which made the gods much too humanly beautiful, too aesthetically satisfactory to be real Powers, and its inner, which robbed the gods of their marvellous potency by representing their interventions in a way comprehensible to men. Seen from the religious point of view this opposition to the aesthetic flattening of religion is quite intelligible and even testifies to the need of a deeper conception of it, but it was the evil destiny of this movement, coming as it did up from the depths of the people and associated with Oriental demonology, to carry with it a primitive stratum of religion and therefore result in sorcery, magic, and belief in demons in our sense.

The Christians had as implicit faith as the heathen in wonders, magic, and daimones, and exorcism found a place in their ritual. They did not deny that the pagan gods could work miracles, but they accounted their actions to be the work of evil daimones and fought those daimones in reliance upon the omnipotence of God; they did not, however, deny them. How terrible the power of belief in demons was a later age showed, for in it Christianity, freed from the struggle against paganism, absorbed a popular element and developed the doctrine of the Prince of Evil and his realm, which for centuries tormented mankind like a nightmare. Christianity also recognized intermediate beings, angels and archangels, who incidentally made their way also into the magical papyri, but these, unlike the pagan daimones, did not occupy a position at least half independent; they did not constitute the kingdom of God but His court; His kingdom was the faithful, humanity. The conception of the fallen angels was an attempt to solve the problem of the existence of evil in a world created by the good God. Although Christianity opposed the belief in daimones, it unfortunately shared it as well.

In conclusion, a few words must be said about the magical papyri which have so often been mentioned in the preceding pages. Those which are preserved come from Egypt, but they existed everywhere. The Acts of the Apostles tell us that when St. Paul preached in Ephesos, his converts collected and burned documents of that kind to the value of 50,000 pieces of silver. The papyri contain magical recipes, conjurations, descriptions of sorceries, and methods for procuring appearances of gods and daimones and predictions of the future. As, in the Black Art of later times, use is made of Christian prayers, among others the Paternoster, the magical texts incorporate a selection of the religion of their day and so are valuable even from the religious point of view. For instance, they contain a prayer which recurs in a Hermetic document; the concluding prayer in the *Poimandres* is found on a papyrus, addressed to the Christian God, for there were no such watertight compartments dividing the religions of late antiquity as we are apt to suppose. The magical papyri give us hymns to the gods in the same style and with the same accumulation of epithets which we know from hymns that have come down from Imperial times; some of these have a certain elevation and are probably borrowed; others, made after the pattern of the former, contain magical components. The magical ceremonies are called mysteries, and the magician a mystagogue or a *mystes*, an initiate.

Such Greek gods as were fit for the purpose are mentioned, Apollo as an oracular deity and Hekate as goddess of witches; since the documents come from Egypt it is obvious that the Egyptian gods occupy a great space, above all the evil god Typhon. The Jewish contribution is very large; Iao (Yahweh) is often mentioned and we find also the Hebrew names of the angels. Oriental deities, on the contrary, are very rare; Mithra and the Babylonian goddess Erishkagil are mentioned a few times. With all these are associated vast quantities of abracadabras, unintelligible words and series of letters, among which the seven vowels of the Greek alphabet take a leading place. Something has already been said of the method of getting an oracle.

The appearance in these texts of two well-known ideas is important for the history of religion. One is that of power. Magicians do not pray but compel gods or daimones by their potency, and the potency (*dynamis*) which the operator assumes is called divine power or spirit (*pneuma*), or divine effluence (*apórrhoia*); sometimes the magician identifies himself with a god.

The other idea is the all-governing position of the highest god of the universe, the god who created and guides the world, under whatever name he appears, for sometimes he is called Helios, sometimes Aion, sometimes he has no name. We may quote a couple of examples of prayers to this God.

I invoke thee, the greatest of all, the creator of all, thee the self-produced, who seest all things and art not seen; for thou gavest the sun his glory and all his power, thou hast made the moon to wax and wane and have her appointed courses; thou tookest nothing away from the darkness that was before but gavest it an equal portion, for at thine appearance the world was and light appeared. Unto thee are all things subject, thou whose very shape none of the gods can see. Thou that art changed into the shapes of all art the invisible Aion of the Aion.

Come to me, thou from the four winds, almighty god, who didst breathe spirits into men that they should live, Master of the fair things in the universe, hear me, O Lord, whose hidden name is unspeakable, which when the daimones hear they cower, which when the sun and the earth hear they turn about, which when Hades hears he is troubled, rivers, the sea, lakes and springs when they hear it are frozen, rocks when they hear it are broken; the sky is thy head, the ether thy body, the earth thy feet, and the water about thee is the Ocean, O Good Daimon. Thou art the Lord who begettest and nurturest and givest increase to all things.

II. THE SOCIAL SIDE

The axiom, so often put forward as a self-evident truth, that religion is a private matter, belongs rather to wishful thinking than to the world of reality. Everyone who has a living religious faith tries to find support and edification with others who share the same faith. Disciples gather around masters, the faithful around a prophet. Herein lies the germ of a community, or, if the faith which is proclaimed constitutes a part somewhat different from the rest of a more general doctrine, the germ of a sect. Not even the most exalted forms of religion can escape such a formation of communities or sects; on the contrary, they are distinguished by a high degree of missionary enthusiasm and of zeal. So it was with Hermetism, in which there are even unmistakable traces to be found here and there of the formation of sects. In the Christian branch of the same movement, Gnosticism, the formation of sects went forward at so excessive a rate that it broke up into more than half a hundred of them.

Such sectarianism, when every prophet opens his mouth to speak and gathers an assemblage of the faithful around him, puts the continuance of the whole movement in danger, for the differences assume greater importance than the things held in common. That is one of the reasons why Gnosticism came off second best in its fight with the Church, which, despite all contrary tendencies, upheld unity and rested upon an organization which included its congregations in the higher common unity. In this period the formation of communities was unaffected by the State's power, whereas in older times religion had become a part of the State and of society. We must turn to the older period and examine how it came about that the communities were formed and organized on the ground of religious belief.

In our introduction it was observed that the ancient Greek religion, that is to say, cult, was the religious side of the activity of the family, the State and its subordinate parts. The same state of things existed in early Rome, which also was a small sovran state, consisting of a city and the surrounding territory. The foundations of this religion were undermined when large political units, the Hellenistic kingdoms, were set up and the little States lost the power of independent political activity and became merely pawns in the game played by the great powers. The extension of the Roman world-power to the Mediterranean countries and the institution by the Empire of an efficient central government is the final result of this development; the once independent States sank to mere communes within the Empire, while their ancient religions lived on merely in the form of local patriotism.

What the new state of the world needed was, from this point of view, a universal, world-wide religion, as all-embracing as the world-Empire. The solution which the older Oriental empires had found, in Egypt, where the Theban Ammon-Rê became the god of the whole kingdom, or in Babylonia, where Marduk of Babylon and afterwards the Assyrian god Assur was put at the head of the world of gods and of the State alike, was not possible for the Roman dominions. Juppiter Optimus Maximus of the Capitol neither reached nor could reach any such position. Cicero's remark, 'Every State has its religion and we have ours', voices a maxim which for the ancients was self-evident. The world of the gods which was contained within the boundaries of the Empire, from the Atlantic to the Euphrates, was miscellaneous and multiform past all description; the ethnical unity which had made it possible for the ancient Eastern empires to subordinate the gods' world under a single national deity was lacking; so far from unity, there was a diversity which could not be unified. The reason for the diversity was that every people within the bounds of the Empire practised its national religion, which in the East rested upon millennial tradition (we may remember the Greeks, Asians, Egyptians, Syrians, and Jews) and upon the constitution of the religions which these peoples embraced.

Imperial Rome made an attempt, which had been foreshadowed in the Hellenistic monarchies, to set up an Empire-wide religion, the cult of the Emperors. If the Roman State, the Empire, looked for a form of religious expression, the Imperial cult was the only one they could find to set forth the feeling of the unity and greatness of the Empire and of loyalty towards it and its ruler. The army, an increasingly miscellaneous assemblage of all manner of peoples, was held together by the *disciplina Romana*, the religious form of which was the cult of the standards and of the Emperor, whereof the former expressed the soldierly virtues, the latter loyalty to the Empire, incarnate in the person of the supreme commander-in-chief. Under the form of Emperor-worship, Augustus gave freedmen and the lower classes, who were excluded from the regular religious observances, an organization which made them loyal partisans of the Empire. In much the same way and by the same means he gave the provinces a cult-organization in which their leading inhabitants could to a certain extent, although within strict limits, be active themselves and not be simply governed from above, and in which they could satisfy their social ambition. Thereby the principal men of the provinces became whole-hearted supporters of the Empire.

Emperor-worship is a masterpiece of the politician's art of employing religion towards the upbuilding of the State, and it contributed to keeping the Empire together; but, like all religious constructions of politicians, it had a weakness, for it lacked all genuine religious content. The ancients were by that time well acquainted with the difference between gods and men, even if the latter were deified and received divine honours; the living Emperor was a human being and those Emperors who had been deified were dead men; it now and then happened that an Emperor was denied that honour. Still, even though the Imperial cult lacked a genuinely religious content, it shows how powerful a good organization can be. Against the religious currents of the time it could make no opposition.

The Romans were, as the Greeks always had been, tolerant in matters of religion. They took it as natural and self-evident that every people had its own, and they had no objection to a foreign religion being embraced by others, provided it did not disturb the peace of society and the constitution of the State. The Oriental religions profited by this freedom, and their spread is the most remarked phenomenon in the religious history of the Empire. They brought with them from their own countries a kind of organization, for they had a professional priesthood, divided into many grades, the higher members of which occupied themselves exclusively in the service of their god and propaganda for his cult. They sought for extension, to some degree for universalism. They endeavoured to exalt their god as high as possible; Isis claimed to unite all deities and their potency in herself. Their limitation was their connexion with a national cult; it was not possible for them, by sacrificing their individual character, to pass into a higher unity such as the age and the condition of the world demanded. Isis, Mithra, the Great Mother with Attis, all lived peaceably alongside each other and in company with the many other gods of the Empire.

The faithful formed congregations and their attachment to the cult was emphasized by duties which were incumbent upon them not only in the mysteries but also in public worship. If they attained complete inclusion in the cult they must assume the outward signs which the national origin of the worship called for; they were adopted as members of the people whose property the cult was. Those who were included in the Jewish communities were circumcised, while those who were received among the servants of Isis shaved their heads as the Egyptians were accustomed to do. Apart from these there were many, probably the great mass of adherents, who associated themselves only part way, without submitting to such requirements, for instance, in Jewish congregations, the so-called 'god-fearing'.

The organization above-mentioned did not extend beyond the individual congregations. There is no indication whatever that the congregations which worshipped a particular god within the same province, still less within the Empire as a whole, co-operated mutually or combined into an association or other organization. If we read Apuleius' account of Lucius' initiations into the mysteries of Isis, first at Corinth and afterwards twice in Rome, carefully, we almost get the impression that the clergy in the one place did not fully recognize the initiation which had been carried out in the other, but imposed a new one.

None of the mystery-religions, on account of their inner nature, could elevate itself to a universal religion; they were and they remained attached to their national origins, even if as a result of their spread among foreigners they adapted themselves to their environment and to changed circumstances. They lacked an organization to bind together the many conventicles in various places in the Empire into a co-operating unity. The attempt which theological speculation made to absorb the different deities in the supreme God, the creator and ruler of the world, had no expression in religious practice and was of no consequence, for every religion retained its own character and made out its own deity to be the highest.

There was, however, one religion which confessed such a god, the cult of the Sun; but Sun-cult, apart from certain worships in Syria, was the learned product of theological and astrological speculation. It has left behind sundry memorials which show that it was glad to associate itself with another deity and had no great importance among the people. It was patronized by the later Emperors, because, as already remarked, it fitted very well with their claims to sovranty and majesty, and when it was officially introduced by the Emperor Aurelian, it was given a place among the ancient worships of Rome and did not create an organization including the whole Empire. It is certain that the prerequisite for any such thing, namely, congregations of sun-worshippers, was lacking.

Judaism, about the time of the Nativity of Christ, carried on a lively propaganda and won many adherents, but would not budge an inch from the Jewish law. After the great

Jewish disturbances, it drew in its horns and ceased from propaganda. The opportunity which Judaism lost was seized upon by Christianity. Christianity was in the true sense a universal religion, rising superior to nations and peoples; for it there was no question of circumcision or uncircumcision, of Jew or Greek or Egyptian, but only of human beings. Christianity taught men to render unto Caesar that which was Caesar's, but it tolerated the states of this world only so long as they were without prejudice to its own domain. The kingdom of God is not of this world, but the kingdom of God is superior to the states constructed by men. There were combustible materials from which a conflict might blaze up.

In religion there dwells a revolutionary power. It appeared in a violent form in the so-called Sibylline oracles, which are of Jewish and Christian origin, which foretold the downfall of Rome, the Last Judgement, the punishment of enemies, and a millennial reign of a communistic kind, in which all class-distinctions were abolished and the earth bore fruit of its own accord. These predictions found ready ears and contributed greatly to the spread of Christianity and the undermining of the authority of the State. There is nothing whatever to indicate that the public authorities knew them and saw how dangerous they were; in the end, the Christian Church had to take up the contest against the fantastic hopes which they awakened. It cost it much trouble to suppress them, but it had to be done, to prevent a break-up. The Christian Church stood out against forces disruptive of society.

The Roman State left religions in peace, but kept an eye upon communities, because these might become breeding-grounds of discontent and disquiet, although many societies led a clandestine existence as unrestrained and illegitimate organizations. This was a point at which conflict with the authority of the State might arise, and did; another was the least religious of all the State ceremonies, Emperor-worship. For to refuse to give formal worship to the Emperor when called upon to do so was a *crimen laesae maiestatis*, conduct calculated to bring the government into contempt, and for a Christian it was out of the question to sacrifice to a false god. In everyday life such an extremity could be avoided, but it sometimes happened that a Christian was brought face to face with it by the magistrates. The easily aroused fanaticism of heathen mobs contributed to the outbreak of a persecution of those who denied the gods, for that was how the Christians appeared to the pagans. Despite this, we have the Christians' own word for it that martyrs were few and easily counted during the first two Christian centuries. The great persecution which was started by the Emperor Diocletian arose from the fact that he, being a mercilessly methodical man in all his dealings, became convinced that Christianity was a danger to and a rival of the power of the Roman State. Fundamentally he was right, but Christianity had already grown so powerful that it was a hopeless undertaking to try to eradicate it.

Its power depended not only on its faith, but also upon the organization which united all Christians, the organization by the help of which the Church succeeded in overcoming Gnosticism, and which was developed and strengthened during the struggles which arose therefrom, and was later also to overpower the disturbances arising from chiliastic expectations. The conflicts had arisen within the Christian community, and it might have seemed a simple solution that the different parties in a community should separate and form each its own community, but this did not happen, for the large-scale social relief work for the benefit of the poor, sick, and needy which the community maintained could not be divided unless it was to lose its value. The community was an indivisible unity, which from the beginning had been led and governed by the president chosen for life by the brethren, the bishop.

The Christian organization was connected with that of the Empire. The Christians in each city and the surrounding district formed a community under a bishop; a division of this was as unthinkable as the existence of two jurisdictions in the same city. The country districts had no congregations but belonged to the congregation in the city, just as their administration was subordinate to that of the city. Communication between congregations was maintained by travelling brethren. From the very start, when the Apostles, prophets, and missionaries were going about, it was the duty of the congregation to receive and maintain these, a duty which was later extended to the leaders of the congregations, when it was necessary for them to meet and take council on matters of common interest. Thus arose, supported by a self-government such as was otherwise denied to the subjects of the Roman Empire, bureaucratically ruled from above as they were, that organization which set at naught the power of the Roman State and, in the shape of the Roman Catholic Church, subjected Europe to itself, in striking contrast to the lack of intercommunication between the congregations of the faithful within the rival pagan religions. Christianity was building the kingdom of God upon earth, and need shed no tears at seeing the barbarians overflow and break the Empire, for it stood above the nations and included the barbarians also in its universalism. It made no mistake in trusting that it would be able to embody even the barbarians in the City of God.

The advance of the Christian Church is an imposing historical drama. The fundamental causes were firm belief in the truth of the Christian religion, universalism, and brotherly love, including its manifestation in the help given the destitute and helpless, also the vitalizing force of self-government in a bureaucratized world; but all that would not have sufficed to construct so vast a work had not the power and ability to organize, which had raised up the world-dominion of Rome, become once more a living and active spirit. Only Christianity could give the Roman world the religious organization which answered its need and its unity, and it gave it.

With the insight of genius, Constantine the Great perceived that Christianity was the one living force which was capable of holding the crumbling Empire together, and that the Christian Church was the one organization which had popular support. He laid his hand on the Christian Church. It is usually said that he recognized Christianity and that that marked its victory, for it was intolerant on principle of those who disagreed with it and it rejected the pagan religions. This is true, but the gain was not all on the side of the Church. The bond between religion and the State was knit anew, the Emperor convoked the Church councils at which doctrinal disputes were settled, and converted their decisions into laws of the Empire. He was *de facto* the *summus episcopus*, and what he thought of his position is best shown by the fact that in the Church of the Apostles at Constantinople, the round building which he had erected to be his mausoleum, he placed his own sarcophagus in the middle with cenotaphs of the Twelve Apostles around it.

Constantine's work laid the foundations for the future. Our view of it is obscured by the fact that the development took a different turn in western Europe. When the Emperors no longer had their seat in Rome, the halo of the Eternal City came instead to illumine the head of its Church, and when the Empire collapsed, the Pope inherited the Imperial claim to power, albeit it was in the City of God, which he governed by the sword of the spirit and his legions of monks. The City of God, in the shape of the Roman Catholic Church, preferred high claims to power over the secular States. But in the East, Constantine's creation stood the test. The Christian religion held the Byzantine Empire together and lent it as long a lease of life as that of Rome from the traditional date of her foundation to Constantine's day. The early loss of Egypt and Syria to the Arabs was due in no small measure to their obstinate adherence to the Monophysite heresy, which cut them off from the ruling State Church and the central government. In the East, down to our own times, the difference between the peoples has not depended upon race, speech or nationality, but upon religion. Soviet Russia has adopted the policy of Constantine, by reviving the patriarchate of Moscow as a means to its ends in the strife of political interests.

It may be asked what this section, which deals with religious organization and State religion, has to do in a discussion of religious feeling. If a religion is one man's private faith, it disappears with him, or else is communicated to others. If so, there arises a community of men of like belief, who look for support and encouragement from one another and are the germ of a religious congregation. Religion and the State may be separated as a result of the conviction that religion is a private business, as has happened in America, but despite this separation, religion remains a powerful social force. So it is in the United States, for no politicians have the fear of God so much in their mouths as the Americans.

Such a separation could not be thought of in antiquity, in which from time immemorial religion had been one of the functions of the State. Ancient religious tolerance was a piece of political wisdom, the result of the necessity of letting the peoples keep their hereditary religions, but it had its limitation; the religions must not disturb the State's activities. If a religion made serious claims to universality, a clash was inevitable. And those who hold the firmest religious faith are the most convinced of their religion's supreme value, and therefore the most intolerant. Such a religion must conquer or die, and if it conquers, it takes the power of the State into its service. Religious feeling lives within these boundaries and takes such expression as the age and circumstances make possible. No one can really understand religion or religious feeling if he does not understand their expression in the actual world. They are eminently factors of society.

CONCLUSION

THE ancient Greek religion was one of Nature, whose gods governed the varying natural phenomena, while others represented the activities of human life or the instincts of mankind. It was from the beginning social or collective. Many peoples have practised such a religion, but in Greece, although in its beginnings it was savage, it became the religion of a great civilization. Therefore its relation to intellectual culture became the greatest religious problem. The intellectual inheritance of the Greeks was their sense of plastic beauty and their gift of clear, logical thought. Their rich intellectual equipment was not lacking in a tendency towards the mystical and ecstatic, which broke forth in the remarkable religious movements of the archaic period as a protest against collective religion, but met with another current which was strong enough to check them, the sense of order and law, sanity and moderation; this current also sprang from human society, from the collectivity. Its highest expression was justice, and the struggle for justice was the *leitmotiv* of the contests of the archaic period; but this was waged in the first place on the social plane. Zeus was the highest defender of justice, but not justice incarnate. In religious feeling there dwelt the attempt to render to the gods what was the gods', and this found expression in a legalism resting on a popular foundation, which sought peace with the gods by regulating human life in the small affairs of every day.

On this foundation Apollo of Delphoi erected his position of leader of the religious life of that time, but Apollo was one of the Olympians, the son of Zeus, a legislator but not a reformer, and did not understand the profundity of the demand for justice. He did his people the service of not troubling about petty, everyday matters, provided the requirements of cult were satisfied, and the substance of his teaching was the only possible one, since the gods did not satisfy the ethical demand, namely, humility, submission without asking for justice or fixed standards in the doings of the gods; *gnothi seautón*. He preached order, sanity, and moderation, and the sages of the time, who were trying to quiet the social conflicts, agreed with his recommendation; *medèn agan*.

The demand for justice led, on the social plane, to a demand for the equal distribution of the good things of life and on the religious, to the idea of an equalization of men's fates, in such a way that a given amount of good luck was counterbalanced by an equal amount of ill luck. This idea found expression in the doctrine of *hybris* and *nemesis*, man's frowardness and the gods' smiting down of the froward. The power which brought about such a levelling was not to be found in individual gods, but only in a general conception of deity, in the divine. This religion of resignation gave neither the support, the hope in tribulation, nor the comfort in sorrow which man looks for from a higher power. Religion came adrift and became an easy prey for the destructive criticism of intellectualism. It survived in its outward forms as a religion of patriotism and, after the states lost their independence, of local patriotism. The gods survived in mythology, literature, and art. The lower forms of religion, belief in beings inhabiting Nature and belief in the shadow-realm of the underworld, have survived even to our own day among the rustic population who were untouched by intellectual culture. The ground was cleared and a new structure must be erected if religious feeling was to find a home, and the spirit of the age determined what the style of that structure should be.

There is a conversion, not of the individual only, but of all humanity, and such a conversion occurred in antiquity. When a man sees his world of concept and thought smashed to pieces and his hopes ruined, repressed powers rise up from the recesses of his soul and guide him on a new path. A new

religious experience may shed a new light on his existence.
The conversion of humanity does not take place all at once,
but needs a long time, for what is changed is the entire
mental atmosphere from which all individuals draw the
spirit which consciously or still more unconsciously deter-
mines their view of life and their outlook on the world, their
activities and their thoughts.

The conversion which humanity underwent in antiquity
was prepared by the collapse of the ancient religion, began
in the middle of the Hellenistic period, and went on with
ever greater strength under the Empire, until it was per-
fected in the victory of Christianity and the passing of the
ancient culture into the Middle Ages. It was a conversion
from rationalism to mysticism, from the clear, logical lines of
Greek thought to faith in the wonderful, supernatural, and
supersensuous, from love of the beauty of the world and the
body to flight from the world and condemnation of all that
was corporeal, from sensual desire to asceticism. The Greek
word `asketés`, which once meant 'athlete', came to mean
'ascetic'. It was a conversion from social or collective piety
to individual religion, for the individual chose his religion
from among the movements of the age, even though he
might seek the fellowship of men of like faith, and so a new
collective piety arose; but it was not associated with society
but with the religious community.

In the above pages mention has been made of the bank-
ruptcy of science and the feeling of weariness which over-
took the educated world at the beginning of the Empire.
To illustrate this side of the spirit of those times I permit
myself to extract a few expressive lines from the ingenious
work of Gilbert Murray, *Five Stages of Greek Religion*, with
a certain reservation, for that celebrated scholar's standpoint
is much the same as that of men of to-day.

[The Hellenistic Age was] a period based on the consciousness of
manifold failure, and consequently touched both with morbidity and
with that spiritual exaltation which is so often the companion of

morbidity. It not only had behind it the failure of the Olympian theology and of the free city-state, now crushed by semi-barbarous monarchies; it lived through the gradual realization of two other failures—the failure of human government, even when backed by the power of Rome or the wealth of Egypt, to achieve a good life for man; and lastly the failure of the great propaganda of Hellenism, in which the long-drawn effort of Greece to educate a corrupt and barbaric world seemed only to lead to the corruption or barbarization of the very ideals which it sought to spread. This sense of failure, this progressive loss of hope in the world, in sober calculation, and in organized human effort, threw the Greek back upon his own soul, upon the pursuit of personal holiness, upon emotions, mysteries and revelations, upon the comparative neglect of this transitory and imperfect world for the sake of some dream-world far off, which shall subsist without sin or corruption, the same yesterday, to-day, and forever.

And again, in the chapter dealing with the religion of late antiquity, which bears the title 'The Failure of Nerve':

Anyone who turns from the great writers of classical Athens, say Sophocles or Aristotle, to those of the Christian era must be conscious of a great difference in tone. There is a change in the whole relation of the writer to the world about him. The new quality is not specifically Christian: it is just as marked in the Gnostics and Mithras-worshippers as in the Gospels and the Apocalypse, in Julian and Plotinus as in Gregory and Jerome. It is hard to describe. It is a rise of asceticism, of mysticism, in a sense, of pessimism; a loss of self-confidence, of hope in this life and of faith in normal human effort; a despair of patient inquiry, a cry for infallible revelation; an indifference to the welfare of the state, a conversion of the soul to God. It is an atmosphere in which the aim of the good man is not so much to live justly, to help the society to which he belongs and enjoy the esteem of his fellow creatures; but rather, by means of a burning faith, by contempt for the world and its standards, by ecstasy, suffering, and martyrdom, to be granted pardon for his unspeakable unworthiness, his immeasurable sins. There is an intensifying of certain spiritual emotions; an increase of sensitiveness, a failure of nerve.

When we ask the reason for this conversion, the usual answer we get at present is that Greece was strangled in the grip of the East, and it is true that the Eastern mentality triumphed over the Hellenic. But how was this possible? During the centuries before the Persian War a strong current of Oriental influence poured over Greece. We see it in art, in the carvings on ivory and the bronzes, and in a whole period of vase-paintings, known as the orientalizing style. The first Greek natural philosophers got their astronomical knowledge from Babylon, and if our acquaintance with this period were not so insufficient, we certainly should discover more Eastern influence still. But on that occasion the Greeks refined the Oriental element which they encountered, re-made it in the Greek spirit, and worked it into Greek culture, the most glorious creation of antiquity and fundamental for all time to come. But when the relations with the East once more grew lively during the Hellenistic period and Oriental influences again poured over Greece in a torrent, the very opposite took place, and that despite the fact that in the meantime, during the height of the classical period, the Greeks had developed science and philosophy and set up an intellectual culture of whose superiority they were well aware and of which they were proud. It might have seemed that they now possessed much greater capabilities than formerly of testing and refining the foreign elements.

With the coming of the Hellenistic period Greece lost her leading position, and the focal points of the intellectual life passed to cities in foreign countries with a non-Greek population, with whom the Greek immigrants became crossed in blood and in spirit. The foreign invasion of Greek culture took place early. The Hellenistic epoch produced numerous famous and important men of Hellenic stock, but also foreigners who acquired important stakes in Greek thought and culture. The founder of the most important philosophic school of the time, Stoicism, was Zenon, a Semite, and the man who towards the end of the period reshaped Stoicism in a way which determined it for the future, Poseidonios, was a Semite also. There is a distinct difference between the Stoicism which these men taught and that which was taught by the Greek Stoics, Kleanthes and Panaitios. Epicurus, on the other hand, was a Greek.

At the beginning of the Roman period, ancient Greece was wasted and bled white, impoverished and depopulated, one of the most insignificant provinces of the Roman Empire. Only one of the important writers of the Imperial age, Plutarch, was a native Greek, and among the Fathers of the Church we can name only Clement, who is called 'of Alexandria' because he worked there, but was born in Athens. The carriers of Greek education came from Asia Minor, Syria, and Egypt; they were non-Greek or at best half-Greek. Let us take the Neoplatonists as examples. Of their forerunners, Numenios was a Semite, Ammonios Sakkas an Egyptian; their founder, Plotinos, was an Egyptian, his successor, Porphyry, was a Phoenician whose original name was Malchos, and Iamblichos, who gave Neoplatonism its final direction towards theosophy and theurgy, was a Syrian. These men, with non-Hellenic blood in their veins, born and bred in the traditions and intellectual atmosphere of their own countries, brought with them, however unconsciously, the decisive foundations for their thinking, which they disguised in Greek forms. This was much more important and had far more effect than the Oriental doctrines and ideas with which the zealously pursued explorations of the syncretism of late antiquity have been chiefly occupied, whereas they mention only in passing and in general terms the nursery in which these ideas grew. And yet this is the most important and decisive feature, for if these ideas and doctrines had not found a favourable and productive soil, they would have withered. But the ground was prepared for them, owing to the thinning out and enfeeblement of the Greek element in the population.

Herodotos describes the clash between East and West as the leading motif in the history of the world, a contest in which the War of Troy was an episode. The city did not fall to the besiegers who surrounded its walls, but only when enemies were got secretly into the town and opened the gates for their comrades.

Let us look at the intellectual position when, at the close of antiquity, Neoplatonism, in the spirit of Iamblichos, tried to gather the powers of paganism for the last struggle with the advancing forces of Christianity, under the banners of occultism and theosophy, whose foremost champion was the Emperor Julian. The higher, educated classes, in so far as they were interested in religion, lay under the influence of Neoplatonism, had themselves initiated into as many mysteries as possible, and embraced a theosophy which passed for philosophy. God and the gods had become potencies or philosophical principles, and the supreme God was transcendent, incomprehensible, unapproachable, so that a second, intermediary god must step in to make the connexion with the world of phenomena. In practice, this religious feeling expressed itself in mysteries, occultism, spiritistic and psychic phenomena, in asceticism, divination, theurgy, which was nothing more than magic making a claim to be religion. Among the masses this tendency passed into magic and sorcery, superstition and old wives' tales. The educated were served with the more refined diet of theurgy; the people got superstition for their daily bread. The morbid spiritual condition on which the above-named phenomena depend is infectious, and it spread widely; they affect those sensitive to them strongly, but the great majority lack the psychic disposition for them and their attitude towards them is one of mistrust and fear. The ecstatic state played a great part in Christianity at the beginning (the spirit of prophecy, speaking with tongues, &c.), but was soon repressed, as were later the social Utopias which go under the name of chiliasm. Metaphysical Christianity, Gnosticism, was put down and the too speculative theology of an Origen suffered in time the same fate. Thus it was that Christianity represented the sane reaction against occultist phantasms and theosophical fogs. It is quite obvious that at that time Christianity shared the belief in wonders, sorcery, and daimones, among which it counted the pagan gods, but it condemned them and offered protection against them.

Religion had entered into partnership with cosmology, for in the last analysis these religious conceptions and speculations were connected with the new picture of the universe which Greek science had created. There is hardly any religion which has not a cosmology and something to say about the origin and arrangement of the universe, even if that generally belongs, as in the archaic Greek religion in particular it did, rather to the domain of mythology than of religion. A problem arose out of it only when people began to investigate and to explain the existence and construction of the world in an intellectual fashion, that is, with the advance of Greek science. The scientific insight into the construction of the universe was more important than the immature attempts to explain it, for the former showed the more clearly how huge and complex the world is and taught that it is governed by inevitable laws. With this insight the old ideas of gods and divinity must be brought face to face. Religion must either adopt or reject the views attained by science.

Pagan religion in late antiquity chose the former road. The clearest example is sun-worship and the astrological conceptions which knit together all the religious forms of that time; Neoplatonic theologians gave cosmological explanations of repellent old myths and cults. Meanwhile, religious transcendentalism forced to the front a transcendental superstructure to the universe; it did not reject the contemporary ideas of how the material world was constructed, but made it out to be the place of evil. This movement bore the name of *gnosis*, and its primitive form is Hermetism. In Christian Gnosticism and in Manicheism, salvation, or deliverance from evil, sometimes turns into a cosmic drama.

Religion forgets its true nature if it occupies itself too much with cosmology, because its kernel is man, not the universe. Christianity had an instinctive feeling for this truth, and supported it by the authority of the Old Testament. The cosmological speculations which the pagan religions and Gnosticism had taken up were learned or semi-learned, the people had no more than a general vague idea of them. We can form some idea of this if we look to see what Christianity adopted and what it rejected, for it could not have attained its wide diffusion and final victory if it had not been in agreement with what the people thought. The people understood the old notion that the souls of the pious after their death went up into the air, but not the journey of the soul through the planetary spheres. It understood that God is enthroned on high and that the souls of the pious gather around Him, but it knew also that the dead exist in their graves and work from them. It understood that the lower world was a place of punishment, but not that souls are purified in the atmosphere. It would, however, be an unpardonable exaggeration to degrade Christianity to the lowest level of the popular belief and to judge it accordingly. The Christian God had His throne in heaven; He was exalted but at the same time personal. He did according to His will and the angels were the bearers of His commands. Christ was a historical figure, with no mythological accretions to burden Him. Entirely through Him, Christianity kept the nearness of God to mankind, but also was caught in a web of Christological controversies, for Christ was in effect a second God, a mediator between God and man, who was God and man at once.

Taken on the whole, Christianity represented the wholesome reaction against the theosophy of late antiquity and won because the majority could not acquire theosophy. Neoplatonism, in its championing of the ancient religion, strayed into a wrong path, for it was much too 'scientific', even though it ranked science much lower than the higher enlightenment. Religion encounters strong influences from science, but forgets its true nature if it tries to take up too much science into its views, which was precisely where Neoplatonism went wrong, despite its openly professed contempt for science.

Christianity has been accused of enmity against science, and in certain Fathers of the Church one can find very strong expressions of such an enmity. However, we must not forget that the moralizing Stoics of the Empire, the Cynics, and the Neoplatonists treated science with the same lack of respect; it is indifferent for a good and happy life, worthless for union with the Supreme Being. The worst of it was that the scientific spirit had disappeared; the Empire lived on the old inheritance, which dribbled on in soulless compilations. What the Neoplatonists called science was scholasticism and theosophy. Sometimes one is tempted to be grateful to Christianity for sweeping these cobwebs away. Here also Christianity represents the healthy reaction, although unfortunately it threw out the baby with the bath-water, as the Swedish proverb has it, and accepted elements of popular belief which, after its victory and under the degenerate educational conditions of the time, spread disastrously, the high value set on asceticism, the cult of relics, belief in Hell and so forth. In short, Christianity won because at bottom it was healthier than the vaporous paganism of late antiquity and because, unlike the old official religions, it offered humanity real religious values. The paganism of late antiquity had too much cosmology in it and too little real religion.

The war waged by paganism against the advance of Christianity was fought on two fronts by two very different classes. One consisted of the common people, who led a simple life, untouched by the movements of the time, and therefore clung to old belief and old custom; these were to be found principally among the country population, while Christianity was distinctly a religion of city-dwellers. Their resistance, though passive, was stubborn and in time compelled the Church to make great concessions. The other class consisted of the educated who indulged in thought about religion.

They could not be content with mere polemic against Christianity but must set up a religious doctrine in opposition to the Christian, to show not only the inferiority of the latter but still more the higher value of the old religion. The sources for this pagan theology are abundant, while the passive resistance of the simple people is mentioned only incidentally and its strength is manifested only by the results. It was not so easy to suppress it by Imperial decrees as it was to put down official paganism. The spiritual warfare rightly stands in the forefront of interest and of investigation. If we go to the bottom of it, it brought about the decisive victory of the new faith. The last effort of ancient paganism under the banners of occultism and theosophy was bound to fail, but it was founded upon a tendency in the depths of the human spirit which always recurs and did recur later, taking such formal expression as the age stamped upon it. But such a current of thought has never reached such vigour and extension as in the last period of antiquity.

Every religion is burdened with much dross and sometimes buried under it. It may be that we must uncover a great deal and dig deep before we can find the life-giving springs, but a living religion has powers which try to wash away the rubbish and let the springs well up. A religion belonging to the past, a dead religion, does not fare so well. Unfriendly hands turn over its rubbish-heap, sort out the pieces of rubble, and examine them to find their origin, and that is labelled science. It is very difficult, indeed impossible, to arouse the living spirit which once throbbed in the frozen forms.

Times change and we change with them; so does religion. Religion must, if it is to satisfy the spiritual needs of humanity, correspond to the age's views of life and the world; in an epoch when science has a decisive influence on man's outlook upon the world and on the universe, religion must take account of the thought of the time, but it forgets its true nature if it tries to adopt too much of a picture of the world which originates from scientific investigation. That was the mistake which paganism made in late antiquity; it had too much cosmology and not enough genuine religion. But it should not merely be blamed; in its best moments it was the expression of an honest search and a profound longing for the highest. I know no better expression of this longing and this search than that in one of the poems of the Swedish poet, Viktor Rydberg; it is called *Whence and whither?*

> Deeper and deeper his (Time's) cable goes;
> Grave after grave, and link on link,
> Still in Infinity's sea they sink,
> Striving each hour, and still in vain,
> Eternity's soundless depths to gain.
> I dreamed through hosts of suns I flew,
> And wandered starry meadows through.
> Alas, each star was a prison-cell
> Where doubt and pain and anguish dwell,
> And moans arose from every one,
> 'Whence come we? Whither must we run?'
> And every ray that lights the sky
> A question is that craves reply.
> But the answer to 'whence and whither we?'
> It lay on silent Darkness' knee.

If it has not been made sufficiently clear from the foregoing account that the eternal question 'whence and whither?' became the deepest problem of late antiquity, let their own religious thinkers bear witness in conclusion.

At the beginning of the first and, in its way, the most remarkable of the Hermetic writings, the *Poimandres*, the disciple explains his wishes to Hermes Trismegistos:

I would learn the things that are, know their nature and get knowledge of God.

That is the programme of Hermetism.

The greatest of the Christian Gnostics, Valentinus, says:

Fate (*heimarméne*), then, is true only until baptism; after that, the astrologers no longer speak truly. But it is not only the lustral water that sets free, but also the enlightenment (*gnosis*) as to who we were, what we are become, where we were or where we have been placed, where we are hastening, from what we are ransomed, what birth is and what rebirth.

Porphyry the Neoplatonist expresses the same thought at such length that his expressions must be summarized. My utterance, he says in effect, is not meant to advise those who lead the practical life, but for one who would consider who he is and whence he came and whither he should hasten; not to him who dreams but to him who would shake off sleep.

Viktor Rydberg finds the answer in his conclusion:

> In dreams my home came back to me;
> I was a child on my mother's knee.
> The question I'd heard from stars above
> Got for answer a kiss of love.
> We gazed and gazed each other upon
> Till all the world save her was gone,
> And boundless space was grown so small
> That her blue eyes found room for all,
> And time stood still, till I could see
> In my mother's look, Eternity.

Christianity gave the same answer. It cast away the cosmological speculations and went back to the old picture of the world. The mystics of late antiquity taught that he who knows his own real nature, he who has *gnosis*, or illumination, is absorbed in God. Christianity substituted a childlike trust in the heavenly Father, 'Our Father, which art in heaven'.

REFERENCES TO ANCIENT AUTHORS

PAGE

1. Herodotos, ii. 53.
3. Hesiod, *Theogony*, 881.
9. Strabo, viii, p. 343.
10. Plutarch, *Non posse suauiter uiui*, 1101e; cf. *De superstitione*, 169d.
10. Aristotle, *Polit.* 1313^b 21 ff.
11. Plutarch, *Pericles*, 12.
12. Theognis, 773 ff.
15. *Anthologia Palatina*, xiv. 71.
24. Plato, *Laws*, iii. 701b; *Cratylus*, 400c; Pindar, fgt. 116 Bowra.
25. Pindar, fgt. 127 Bowra, from Plato, *Meno*, 81b–c; *Olymp.* ii. 62 ff.; Euripides, fgt. 638 Nauck; Plato, *Gorgias*, 492e.
28. Nilsson, *History of Greek Religion*, trans. F. J. Fielden, p. 222.
29. Empedokles, fgt. 112 (Diels, *Fragmente der Vorsokratiker*, ed. 3, Berlin, 1912).
31. Hesiod, *Works and Days*, 276 ff., 204 ff., 174 ff.
35. Ibid. 252 ff.
36. Anaximandros, fgt. 9 Diels; Aeschylus, *Choephoroe*, 313 ff.
37. Aeschylus, *Agamemnon*, 750 ff.
38. Solon, fgt. 13 (Bergk) = 1 (Diehl), 29; Theognis, 731 ff.
40. Aristophanes, *Frogs*, 448 ff.; Hesiod, *Works and Days*, 242 ff., 225 ff.
43. Aelian, *Varia Historia*, iii. 43; Thucydides, i. 126 ff.
44. Herodotos, vi. 86.
48. Plato, *Protagoras*, 343b; *Charmides*, 164d–e; Pindar, *Isthmians*, 5. 13; Porphyry, *De abstinentia*, ii. 15 ff., from Theophrastos.
50. [Plato], *Hipparchus*, 229a, b.
53. Solon, fgt. 8 (Bergk) = 5 (Diehl), 9; Theognis, 605 ff.
54. Herodotos, i. 207, 2; Theognis, 373 ff., 743 ff.
55. Sophokles, *Aiax*, 127 ff.; Pindar, *Pythians*, 3. 81. 59.
56. Herodotos, i. 1 ff.; iii. 39 ff.
57. Ibid. i. 34, 1; vii. 10e. Herakleitos, fgt. 103 (Bywater) = 43 (Diels); Aristotle, *Rhetoric*, ii. 8, 1385^b; Pindar, *Isthm.* 7. 39; *Pyth.* 10. 20.
58. Herodotos, i. 32.
59. Ibid. vii. 50.
63. Sophokles, *Electra*, 1306; fgt. 653 Pearson.
64. Euripides in Lydus, *De mensibus*, iv. 7, p. 72 Wuensch.
65. Thucydides, ii. 64. 2.
67. Ibid. 38.
74. Xenophanes, fgts. 15 and 11 Diels.

PAGE

75. Euripides, *Ion*, 437 ff. Euripides, fgt. 292 Nauck; Herakleitos, fgts. 130, 128 (Bywater) = 5 (Diels).

76. Prodikos, fgt. B 5 Diels. Demokritos, fgt. A 75 Diels; Kritias in Nauck, *Tragicorum Graecorum Fragmenta* (ed. 2), p. 771.

77. Xenophon, *Memorabilia*, i. 4. Plato, *Laws*, x. 885*b*.

79. Plutarch, *Pericles*, 6.

81. Protagoras, fgt. 4 Diels.

82. Plato, *Apology*, 18, 19*b*.

83. Demokritos, fgt. 297 Diels.

86. Philemon, fgt. 137 Kock; Menander, fgt. 482 Kock.

90. Polybios, vi. 56. 10–12.

98. Petronius, *Satura* 39.

104. Plutarch, *Aetia physica*, 916*d*.

106. Moschopoulos, introd. to scholia on Hesiod, *Works and Days* (p. 33 Gaisford) = Jacoby, *Fragmente der griechischen Historiker*, fgts. 244 and 352 of Apollodoros.

116. Xenophanes, fgt. 23 Diels.

117. Dion Chrysostom, *Orat.* xxxi. 11; Maximus of Tyre, xvii. 5.

118. [Aristotle,] *De mundo*, 397^b 9 ff.

122. Kern, *Orphicorum fragmenta*, fgt. 168.

123. Ibid., fgt. 245; Acts 17. 22 ff.

128. *Corpus Hermeticum*, xiii. 3.

129. Ibid. v. 2; xiii. 2–4.

132. Plotinos, *Enneades*, vi. 7.

143. Migne, *Patrologia graeca*, lxv, p. 313*c*, *d*.

156. Aristotle, fgt. 45 Rose. Dion Chrysostom, *Orat.* xii. 35.

157. Themistios in Stobaios, v, p. 1089 Hense; Apuleius, *Metamorphoses*, xi. 23. Proklos, *In Alcibiadem*, p. 39 Creuzer; *Theol. Plat.* i. 3, p. 7 Portus.

159. Sallustius, *De dis et mundo*, 4, p. 6, 26 Nock.

160. Porphyry in Eusebios, *Praeparatio euangelica*, iii. 12, 4.

165 f. Ammianus Marcellinus, xix. 12, 19; xix. 12; xviii. 3; xxix. 1.

166. Iamblichos, *De mysteriis*, iii. 17.

168. Philostratos, *Heroicus*, 3, 2; Dion Chrysostom, *Orat.* xii. 60 ff.

169. Cf. Plotinos, *Enneades*, iv. 3. 11; Arnobius, *Aduersus gentes*, vi. 17, p. 229. 12 Reifferscheid.

175. *Papyri graecae magicae*, ed. Preisendanz, xiii. 62 ff.; xii. 238 ff.

177. Cicero, *Pro Flacco*, 69.

188 f. G. G. A. Murray, *Five Stages of Greek Religion*, pp. 18, 155.

197 f. Clement of Alexandria, *Excerpta Theodoti*, 78.

198. Porphyry, *De abstinentia*, i. 27.